AFFECTIVE MEDIEVALISM

Series editors: Anke Bernau and David Matthews
Series founded by: J. J. Anderson and Gail Ashton
Advisory board: Ruth Evans, Patricia C. Ingham, Andrew James Johnston, Chris Jones, Catherine Karkov, Nicola McDonald, Sarah Salih, Larry Scanlon and Stephanie Trigg

Manchester Medieval Literature and Culture publishes monographs and essay collections comprising new research informed by current critical methodologies on the literary cultures of the Middle Ages. We are interested in all periods, from the early Middle Ages through to the late, and we include post-medieval engagements with and representations of the medieval period (or 'medievalism'). 'Literature' is taken in a broad sense, to include the many different medieval genres: imaginative, historical, political, scientific, religious. While we welcome contributions on the diverse cultures of medieval Britain and are happy to receive submissions on Anglo-Norman, Anglo-Latin and Celtic writings, we are also open to work on the Middle Ages in Europe more widely, and beyond.

Titles Available in the Series

7. *Rethinking the* South English Legendaries
   Heather Blurton and Jocelyn Wogan-Browne (eds)
8. *Between earth and heaven: Liminality and the Ascension of Christ in Anglo-Saxon literature*
   Johanna Kramer
9. *Transporting Chaucer*
   Helen Barr
10. *Sanctity as literature in late medieval Britain*
    Eva von Contzen and Anke Bernau (eds)
11. *Reading Robin Hood: Content, form and reception in the outlaw myth*
    Stephen Knight
12. *Annotated Chaucer bibliography: 1997–2010*
    Mark Allen and Stephanie Amsel
13. *Roadworks: Medieval Britain, medieval roads*
    Valerie Allen and Ruth Evans (eds)
14. *Love, history and emotion in Chaucer and Shakespeare: Troilus and Criseyde and Troilus and Cressida*
    Andrew James Johnston, Russell West-Pavlov and Elisabeth Kempf (eds)
15. *The* Scottish Legendary: *Towards a poetics of hagiographic narration*
    Eva von Contzen
16. *Nonhuman voices in Anglo-Saxon literature and material culture*
    James Paz
17. *The church as sacred space in Middle English literature and culture*
    Laura Varnam
18. *Aspects of knowledge: Preserving and reinventing traditions of learning in the Middle Ages*
    Marilina Cesario and Hugh Magennis (eds)
19. *Visions and ruins: Cultural memory and the untimely Middle Ages*
    Joshua Davies
20. *Participatory reading in late-medieval England*
    Heather Blatt
21. *Affective medievalism: Love, abjection and discontent*
    Thomas A. Prendergast and Stephanie Trigg

Affective medievalism
Love, abjection and discontent

THOMAS A. PRENDERGAST AND STEPHANIE TRIGG

Manchester University Press

Copyright © Thomas A. Prendergast and Stephanie Trigg 2019

The right of Thomas A. Prendergast and Stephanie Trigg to be identified as the author of this work has been asserted by them in accordance with the Copyright, Designs and Patents Act 1988.

Published by Manchester University Press
Altrincham Street, Manchester M1 7JA, UK
www.manchesteruniversitypress.co.uk

British Library Cataloguing-in-Publication Data is available

ISBN 978 1 5261 2686 3 hardback
ISBN 978 1 5261 4799 8 paperback

First published by Manchester University Press in hardback 2019

This edition published 2020

The publisher has no responsibility for the persistence or accuracy of URLs for any external or third-party internet websites referred to in this book, and does not guarantee that any content on such websites is, or will remain, accurate or appropriate.

Typeset by Out of House Publishing

To our parents

Contents

Acknowledgements *page* viii

Introduction: Medieval and medievalist practice   1
1 The space of time and the medievalist imaginary 22
2 Wonderful things 50
3 Fear, error and death: The abjection of the Middle Ages 70
4 Loving the past 95
5 Discontent in the age of mechanical reproduction 118

Bibliography 134
Index 148

Acknowledgements

We've thought a lot about collaboration while working on this book. We've even given talks on how our collaboration works. But the reality is that we're still not sure. At its best it's a kind of magic where there is no mine and thine, but just 'ours' – acts of friendship and intellectual companionship that are mutual and lasting gifts. Of course, we weren't alone in these happy exchanges. Warm thanks must go to Terry, Paul, Charles and Joel for their kindness, good cheer and smart, loving interrogations. Memorable meetings and conversations with John Ganim, Tom Goodmann and Frank Grady helped us grasp the nature of what we were trying to say; Patty Ingham read an earlier version and gave us robust and helpful feedback; and we are also grateful to David Wallace at the University of Pennsylvania, the BABEL Working Group and the New Chaucer Society for giving us the space and audiences to try out some of these ideas. We published two essays as we developed the book, and are grateful to David Lawton and the other editors of *New Medieval Literatures* and to Liz Scala and Sylvia Federico, editors of *The Post-Historical Middle Ages* for their interest in this project. We owe a special debt of gratitude to the always gracious Carolyn Dinshaw, with whom we have been delighted to engage in debate over a number of years. Anke Bernau and David Matthews have been fantastically welcoming and supportive editors, and the readers for the Press also helped us sharpen the book in a variety of ways. Helen Hickey and Anne McKendry helped us prepare the manuscript with great patience and speed, and Haydie Gooder compiled the index. We express our warm thanks to Andrey Remnev for permission to reproduce his wonderful painting, *Separation of Braids*, on the front cover. For all this support, we are deeply grateful.

Introduction: Medieval and medievalist practice

The old chair

We begin with the critical reception of a chair, an ordinary object that escaped notice for over six hundred years. Only in 1989, at the height of what are somewhat portentously called the theory wars, did a noted critic of medieval literature, Derek Pearsall, turn his attention to this medieval chair, and with it an old problem: the relationship between literary and historical method, and the hermeneutic complexity of reading medieval texts. He isolated a compelling moment in the narrative of the Rising of 1381 – a fragment of text from the *Anonimalle Chronicle* in which a bill prepared by King Richard's clerks was read to the Commons: 'And he caused it to be read to them, the man who read it standing up on an old chair above the others so that all could hear.'¹ In Pearsall's analysis, 'this has the air of something seen, not invented: the arbitrariness of the old chair carries authenticity'.² Pearsall characterises his encounter with this representation of the medieval past as if it were in some sense already informed by our customary familiarity with that past. Being a careful critic, however, he admits that the old chair might well be more ideological invention than authentic detail.³ It was possible that the chronicler was signalling a new era of feudal relations by having the king's representative improvise a new speaking position by climbing up on the 'old' past.

Calling attention to the customary, but arbitrary, distinction between 'historical' and 'literary' ways of reading and studying the past, Pearsall shows how this distinction is both shaky at the level of method, and even more unstable when it comes to assessing the truth of historical sources. Chroniclers such as Froissart, for instance, may have freely invented whole episodes. Pearsall is nevertheless unwilling to surrender completely to the hermeneutics of suspicion. As he writes, 'in the midst of these fantasies of "theory-impregnated" image-making it is necessary to recall that all of these chroniclers are describing an actual event and that at the heart of all of their accounts must be some stubborn, irreducible core of actuality'.[4] His assertion about the actuality of the past and our ability to recuperate it, whether we use the 'modes of understanding' customary to either historical or literary study, is twinned with his insistence that both modes need to recognise 'the shaping power of interpretative models'.[5]

Pearsall was addressing what Cary Wolfe would later describe as the 'modes and protocols by which ... [historical] materials are disciplined' and 'given form'.[6] Pearsall's residual claim about the authenticity of the old chair speaks not just to the epistemological relations between literary and historical method. It is also relevant to more recent discussions as to the ways historical texts and objects can both express their own time, and also express what Paul Strohm calls 'multiple and contradictory temporalities'. Strohm urges 'a refined appreciation of the unruly multiplicity of ways in which history can manifest itself within a text'.[7] We think that invitation might be extended to consider the unruly variety of relationships between the medieval past and post-medieval versions of that past.

As a curious, affective hook for modern readers, the old chair feeds the desire shared by the historical and medievalist imagination to feel, touch and see the medieval past in all its dramatic immediacy, whether that impulse is creative or more scholarly. This episode certainly appeals to the archivist's excitement about seeing an authentic source in an authentic context: the moment when one medieval document (the king's bill) appears embedded in another (the chronicle); and when that same document is also being handled by a medieval body in front of other medieval bodies. But such detail also helps us imagine and 'see' the medieval: and this is the work of the medievalist imaginary.

This chair is a powerful token of the past because it is old in an 'unruly multiplicity' of ways. The chair was old when it was medieval, but it is now also old because it was medieval. If it was already old in 1381 it also invites inevitable comparison with the oldness of chairs in 2018. A chair now might be 'old' because it is aged and shabby, and out of fashion; but it might also be a treasured heirloom with strong family or personal associations. It might be a desirable object of heritage value, a rare antique survival or an item of retro fashion. Or it might be 'old' in even more contradictory ways. It might be a cunning product of medievalism, such as the 'Sussex' and 'Rossetti' rush-seated chairs produced by William Morris in the 1860s. These medieval-style chairs were among the most affordable and most popular items in his company's catalogue. They were sold for as little as 10 or 15 shillings, making it relatively easy for consumers to share in the flourishing global business of medievalism in household design, an early example of the modern heritage economy.[8] These chairs have now become valued museum pieces, yet chairs in this style are also mass-produced for contemporary consumers desiring a taste – and the touch – of the 'old'. This is a form of desire we think has many affinities with the chronicler's pleasure in the old chair.

Old chairs are like old books, old textiles, old songs, old buildings and old stories in that they carry strong affective loads for anyone interested in the medieval past, whether that interest is scholarly or amateur, and whether it is driven by historically oriented scholarship or the desire to possess, or to make, something medieval. Pearsall never mentions medievalism, of course. He uses this chair as a point of focus to think about the relationship between literary and historical method; we invoke it to reconfigure the relationship between medieval and medievalist studies, to suggest that despite many appearances to the contrary, both formations often share a similar desire to 'touch' and 'feel' the past in some way. Moreover, we argue, and hope to show, that the practices and desires of medievalism can help us see more clearly some of the customary distinctions and practices of medieval studies, and how much both formations share in common, especially in the traditions and practices of English literary studies. Here, for example, Pearsall's 'historical' and 'literary' approaches each owe something to what might be called a recuperative method normally associated with 'medieval studies', and a recreative method normally associated with 'medievalism'.

Through the desire to help modern students picture, feel and see the Middle Ages, medieval studies has always been served up with a healthy dollop of medievalism (even if its practitioners haven't always recognised this to be so). Both disciplines deal with a period called the Middle Ages (even if it's not completely clear when that was), and both are activated by a desire to connect in some way with this period. For many decades, the difference between the two disciplines has seemed to be this: while medievalism embraced playful, desirous, imaginative and creative practices, medieval studies (or at least its historicist strand) sometimes believed that our desire to recover the past, and the medieval meaning of medieval things, could be satisfied without reference to the post-medieval imagination. Yet, in the recent review essay on historicism and historicity we have already quoted, Paul Strohm has sensibly echoed what a number of medievalists have been saying for some time now: however we might 'try and try' to recuperate the past, we will never be able to 'get it right'.[9] There will always be what Patricia Ingham has labelled a 'non-convergence' between the truth of the historical event and the knowledge that we produce about the event.[10] But far from indulging in a kind of melancholic hermeneutics, Ingham, Strohm and, notably, Aranye Fradenburg have suggested that we should embrace this state of affairs. As Strohm puts it, the knowledge that 'there's no finality in our interpretations, that we never nail it once and for all … is freeing, in its way',[11] for it enables our desire for the past to continue rather than terminate in some dead end of satisfaction. In practical terms this makes perfect sense, for it enables us to take pleasure in and vitalise the study of the Middle Ages at a moment when both pleasure and vitality are sorely needed. But framing our love and desire for the past in such a negative way seems problematic. As Ingham has suggested, even as we acknowledge the impossibility of producing an account of the past that is objectively true, we always seem to need to act 'as if' an objectively truthful account might be possible.[12]

One could certainly explain this 'as if' by calling it an 'enabling fiction', or by perhaps turning to an ideology of cynicism, a kind of ironic response of an enlightened false consciousness.[13] To put Peter Sloterdijk's idea of 'cynical reason' in medievalist terms, we know very well that the past can never truly be recuperated in all its historical specificity, yet medieval scholarship continues to act as if we are able to recover that past; and is often quick to criticise when medievalist projections appear to get it wrong. The past in this formulation is fantasmatic, projected but seemingly not, in a traditional historical sense, coincidental with the actual past.

So is this projection, that which occasions our desire even before we have attempted to satisfy it, simply false, or, less harshly, merely fictional? Ingham characterises it instead as 'misrecognition' – an impossible fantasy of possession – and Fradenburg suggests it as a 'prop' for desire.[14] We don't desire the object of desire. What we really desire, or rather what desire desires, is 'to keep on desiring'.[15] This move to an abstraction of desire certainly seems tenable in a descriptive sense. And, as Strohm points out, it might be seen as a good thing because it guarantees the continuation of medieval studies, along with all its ongoing institutional, disciplinary and pedagogic practices, and its well-established social identities. But as a call to arms, it seems a bit less persuasive. Even if medievalists

Introduction

are unconsciously motivated by the endless deferral of desire, this is hardly a reason to encourage others or a convincing argument to enlist support for our work. In any case, the move to abstraction seems to elide the very historical particularities that make the work of medievalists like Fradenburg, Ingham and Strohm so compelling.

We advocate instead a more local – and personal – treatment of historicity, suggesting that if desire is motivated by a fantasmatic projection (the object of desire), then in the case of medievalism that projection perversely appears to be available to the desiring subject even before the subject attempts to discover it: this is the vision of medievalism that holds the medieval past always already available for cultural and imaginative recuperation. Such a vision precedes and informs the medieval even before we begin to pursue it in scholarly or creative ways.

Not everyone will agree with this vision of medievalism and the ontological priority we claim for it. To suggest that medievalism might be the pretext to the medieval is to invert the traditional view that the medieval is the starting-point of both the modern and the medievalist. It was, of course, Umberto Eco who first suggested a taxonomy of plural medievalisms, in his tremendously influential distinction between ten competing or variant representations of the Middle Ages: 'every time one speaks of a dream of the Middle Ages, one should first ask which Middle Ages one is dreaming of'.[16] Eco combines his hortation with an injunction that one must choose from his list of 'ten little Middle Ages'. To ignore his list is to fail to do our 'moral and cultural duty'. He expands on what this means when he says that 'to say openly which of the above ten types we are referring to means to say who we are and what we dream of'.[17] While Eco's taxonomy is, presumably, somewhat ironic, it has often been taken as a warning not to conceal who we are and what our (finitely numbered) dreams are for ourselves as well as other people. Behind Eco's playful injunction is a healthy suspicion of the use of the medieval – a belief that the ideological history of the medieval (what he calls at one point the new Aryanism) necessitates an openness that is fulfilled only if we know precisely, even before we speak of the Middle Ages, what we mean by the term.

And in many ways he was prescient about the dangers inherent in the uses of the Middle Ages. Medieval myths, narratives, images and heraldic insignia are regularly co-opted by white supremacist groups wanting to promote the medieval past as a period of racial homogeneity or 'purity'. In the United States, the medieval has been invoked to legitimate the horrific deeds of the Ku Klux Klan. More recently, the so-called Alt-right has adopted symbols derived from the Holy Roman Empire and rhetoric supposedly borrowed from the First Crusade to advance their agenda of white supremacy. These more recent uses of the medieval have even led the normally apolitical Medieval Academy of America to condemn officially the abhorrent uses of the medieval as baseless fantasy: 'As scholars of the medieval world we are disturbed by the use of a nostalgic but inaccurate myth of the Middle Ages by racist movements in the United States. By using imagined medieval symbols, or names drawn from medieval terminology, they create a fantasy of a pure, white Europe that bears no relationship to reality. This fantasy not only hurts people in the present, it also distorts the past.'[18] There is no question that this use of the medieval is horrific. And there is also no question that white supremacists have no idea just how incredibly diverse the Middle Ages was. But for us it is puzzling that the Academy would base its condemnation on the fact that this view of the Middle Ages 'bears no relationship to reality'. The real problem with white supremacy is not that it didn't exist (even if it didn't), but that it is ethically wrong. Plenty of things actually did occur in the Middle Ages that we would, presumably, disavow.

So why would the Academy fall back on the distinction between fantasy and reality in order to legitimate what has been seen as an ethical truism? We might get a hint if we look back at Eco's list of Middle Ages, where hidden within his taxonomy is a privileged actor. Number eight on Eco's list of 'ten little Middle Ages' is 'the Middle Ages of *philological reconstruction* ... which help us ... to criticise all the other Middle Ages that one time or another arouse our enthusiasm'.[19] Eco is far from engaging in a simplistic distinction between a stable Middle Ages and different variable and partial elements of medieval culture that are emphasised by different groups of game-players, fiction-writers, film-makers and so on. But he certainly acknowledges the force of medieval studies as a critique of other examples of medievalism.

In what might be called 'professional academic circles' it has recently become fashionable to abjure such critique, in favour of a more tolerant understanding of creative and amateur medievalism. The academic landscape of the relationship between these fields is currently in process of radical change.[20] There are many versions of medievalism studies that are not grounded in medieval studies as a primary discipline. Conversely, in recent years, medieval scholars have become far less anxious in print and formal academic discourse about the historical accuracy of creative medievalist fictions and films.[21] Nevertheless, the dominant discourse about medievalism is still an epistemological one: how do different groups process the truth about the Middle Ages? After all, the pleasurable impulse of the pedagogic and academic drive to correct mistakes never goes away, whether this is structured by the disciplinary regimes of the academy or driven by the hard-won expertise of the amateur medievalist, fiction-writer and film-maker for whom historical accuracy can be equally compelling.[22] Hilary Mantel, for example, has recently been critical of 'women writers who want to write about women in the past, but can't resist retrospectively empowering them. Which is false.'[23]

At the same time, the continued popularity of Eco's oneiric formulation ('Dreaming the Middle Ages') suggests that the many subsequent variations on 'making', 're-making', 'inventing' and 're-inventing' the Middle Ages have their basis in fantasy work. These re-makings gesture towards a doubled sense that the Middle Ages belong both to the past, as a phenomenon to be interpreted and studied; but also, in a more active sense, to the present, as a phenomenon that is always in process of being re-made. The subtitle of Tison Pugh and Angela Weisl's recent account of the field, *Medievalisms: Making the Past in the Present*, is a typical formulation.[24] The sense that the Middle Ages can be *made*, over and over again, has certainly been an enabling dynamic for modern fantasists who can see themselves as part of a long-standing historical tradition of medievalism that goes back at least as far as the nineteenth century. This tradition is enabling, rather than forbidding; it encourages repetition and rehearsal, rather than interpretative closure, or anything resembling 'the last word' on the medieval past. In this, too, medievalism resembles academic medieval studies. As with all academic fields, to declare its work might be complete would be tantamount to institutional and disciplinary suicide. And, in fact, more recent iterations of the connection between 'medievalism' and medieval studies suggest that the latter depends on the former to perpetuate itself: as David Matthews writes, 'what tends to happen over time is that medieval studies passes into medievalism; as it ceaselessly updates itself, medieval studies expels what it no longer wishes to recognize as part of itself'.[25] It becomes harder and harder, for example, not to see the critical and ideological reception of Chaucer's works as an important document in the history of medievalism.

More radically, others have noted that this medievalist cycle need not be seen only in terms of abjection, but might actually reveal that 'over time, the stated professionalism of medieval studies tends to reveal itself as a subset of medievalism studies'.[26] In temporal terms, then, attempts to recuperate the medieval 'now' will at some future time be seen as less reflective of the Middle Ages and more reflective of the age in which the recuperation took place. Eco's Middle Ages of 'philological reconstruction' can then find its place *in time* within a list of medievalisms. It is a commonly held view that attempts to recuperate the Middle Ages tell us more about those doing the recuperating than the recuperated object. But is this right? It suggests a kind of endlessly regressive vision of literary and historical studies, if all views of our attempts to see, hear and feel the Middle Ages become merely mirrors of the moment when we attempted to reach out and 'touch the past'.[27]

Of course, there are different versions of medievalist practice. In 2005, one of us made the case for at least three forms of medievalism: traditional, modernist and postmodernist. Traditional medievalism is characterised by a 'sensibility [that] assumes that the meaning of this (medieval) object is palpably present to us, both then and now, through an unbroken lineage of embodied or ritualistic connection'. Here, continuity with the past is privileged. By contrast, modernist medievalism typically takes the form of reconstruction. 'Even if they romanticise the content of a "medieval past", modernists, or neo-traditionalists, in comparison to traditionalists, tend to be already modern in form, appealing to historiography, empiricism (much of medieval studies), and antiquarianism (Spenser).' By contrast, postmodernist medievalism manifests as 'an ironical reference or … romanticising pastiche, often condemned as ahistorical or simply "wrong" by old-fashioned historicists'.[28] But the most radical expression of such disconnect of medievalism from the period from which it takes its name has to be what many commentators describe as neomedievalism. Here we mean not so much the political neomedievalism that is described by Bruce Holsinger as 'an argumentative mode' in political theory, where it refers to contemporary projections of a Middle Ages of 'fragmented jurisdictions, amorphous violence, and pre-national sovereignty'.[29] Rather, we refer here to a kind of para- or meta-medievalism that borrows, uses and deploys other medievalisms rather than claiming any direct connection to the Middle Ages.

Neomedievalism tends to be associated even more strongly than medievalism with mass and popular culture, and digital media, and this is a further potential source of division and disconnection from the tactile 'real' world of the medieval archive (a book, a manuscript, a building, an old chair). Further, neomedievalist works, in the words of Harry Brown, 'foster the commodification and mass consumption of the past rather than the earnest attempt to recover and understand it'.[30] Neomedievalist scholars argue that, since the proper object of study for neomedievalism is other medievalisms, neomedievalism constitutes a field separate from traditional studies in medievalism. So, for instance, Brian Helgeland's *A Knight's Tale*, with its deliberate anachronisms (medieval courtiers rocking to the music of Queen, the invocation of the Nike swoosh on William Thatcher's armour), 'spurns nostalgia in preference for a "new and improved alternate universe"'.[31]

One could certainly reject nostalgic longing for the past in the study of works like *A Knight's Tale*, but, as we have shown elsewhere, it's well to remember that such works are often not only the product of a desire to connect with the past, but a belief that such connection is possible.[32] Critics might debate what this is and how it works, but it is important to acknowledge, at least, the pervasive nature of medievalism.[33]

As might be apparent, the impulses governing the different forms of scholarship and activity in this field vary widely. Andrew Cole, Bruce Holsinger, D. Vance Smith and others are deeply interested in how the Middle Ages informs the theoretical and philosophical foundations of modernity and postmodernity.[34] Neomedievalists tend to be interested in a kind of technological presentism. Many practitioners of modern medievalism are often more descriptive – focusing on how particular instantiations of romantic, modern and contemporary medievalism function as representations or ideological arguments within a particular period; while some scholars simply insist on the importance of tradition and continuity with the medieval past. With so many different agendas, ways of working and even different critical objects it seems impossible to think of a singular 'medievalism'. But we think that all these forms share a kind of family resemblance – in their uneasy and sometimes discontented dialectic between past and present – that is more significant than the ways in which they vary.

For us, much of the uneasiness produced by medievalism results from uncertainty about the relationship between the past and the present. Paradoxically, this uncertainty is the result of the very claim that medievalism makes on the past (that is, whether or how it is connected with that past). Further, within various examples of medievalism there is often a meta-moment in which the particular instance of medievalism reveals its own anxiety about such claims. Perhaps unsurprisingly, these moments often reference affect – drawing attention to the circumstances surrounding the reception of the work itself. The mention of the old chair is one such moment. It conjured something memorable for the medieval chronicler; and for us too, it pleats the temporal gap between what 'old' might look and feel like in the fourteenth and the twenty-first century.

'What now?' Medievalism and the uncanny

The possibilities of affective relationships with the past and their connections to knowledge and historical understanding were famously explored by Carolyn Dinshaw in her treatment of the idea of 'getting medieval' (from Quentin Tarantino's 1994 film *Pulp Fiction*).[35] But it is easy to forget the embedded narrative context of Marcellus's suggestion that he was going to 'git medieval on your ass'.[36] It comes in response to a question from his erstwhile saviour, Butch: 'what now?' After Marcellus's response that he is going to 'git medieval' on 'hillbilly boy's ass', after he is raped in an S/M 'dungeon', Butch responds, 'I meant what now between me and you?' Marcellus's response, 'Oh, that what now. I tell you what now between me and you. There is no me and you.'[37] The scene clearly makes manifest the homoerotic implications between Butch and Marcellus and focuses on the break between them as a break-up. But it also invokes the 'what now' inherent in the 'between'. This invocation of temporality as a space 'in the middle' works on two levels. It suggests the impossibility of separating the 'now' from the in between, but it also suggests that for there to be a between there needs to be the 'you and me' that, as Marcellus suggests, still exists between him and 'hillbilly boy'. It is in this space that Marcellus is able to 'get medieval'. Here, as Dinshaw shows, the implications of 'getting medieval' are indeed troubling.

Dinshaw tells us 'the medieval … is the space of the rejects – really the abjects – of the world'.[38] 'Getting medieval' is 'go[ing] to work on homes here with a pair of pliers and a blowtorch', comparable to the provisions of torture prescribed in the thirteenth-century *Li livres jostice et de plet*. This similitude between the now and the then is rich material for us, as this likeness of medievalism

Introduction

and the medieval invites us to consider the relationship between them. At times they appear very similar, but is it truly possible to collapse the two formations? Even Dinshaw, we think, voices some hesitation here, claiming that the twentieth-century torture that is described as 'getting medieval' is 'rather like' thirteenth-century torture.[39] She gives expression to one of the central tenets of what Sigmund Freud describes as 'das Unheimlich' or the uncanny. Freud characterises the uncanny as 'nothing new or strange, but something that was long familiar to the psyche and was estranged from it only through being repressed'.[40] The experience of the uncanny hinges on a kind of intellectual hesitation (*Unsicherheit*) when the subject returns to the familiar that has been repressed, and experiences the profound ambivalence that links the *Heimlich* to the *Unheimlich*. In such moments, other oppositions begin to break down as well. As Elisabeth Bronfen puts it, 'whether something is real or imagined, unique, original or a repetition, a copy, can not be decided'.[41] For Dinshaw this 'dungeon' is peculiarly 'now' and yet '*rather* like' the past (our emphasis). Her hesitation here has much to do with the way that this setting participates in a gothic sensibility. The trappings of the medieval (dungeons, chains, torture devices) are here, but this is not meant to be a medieval setting. One dominant version of gothic, as one of us has put it elsewhere, is 'a non-historical sensibility, a mode of consciousness preoccupied with the repressed'.[42] The medieval here exists under the sign of all that is irrational and primitive. As modern subjects it is absolutely crucial to distinguish ourselves from the medieval and yet there often arises an uncanny and uncomfortable recognition that we are not so different after all.[43]

Medievalists have long understood the power of the uncanny to describe aspects of the medieval period.[44] The *Unheimlich* is often used as a convenient shorthand to signify the profound alterity of the Middle Ages even as the medievalist makes it clear that this alterity somehow makes us feel at home. Yet, in his analysis of the Middle English household imaginary, D. Vance Smith puts his finger on why this concept is so powerful when he says that the experience of the uncanny is 'that which threaten[s] to undo the self'.[45] The ability of the self to define itself, indeed to exist, always relies on the ability of the other to oppose the self and say what it is not. But in the case of the uncanny one cannot decide whether the other is actually strange or familiar. The strange familiarity of the Middle Ages is particularly problematic because it destabilises our sense of time and the changes it might or might not have wrought.

The problem is our understanding of what we call the 'now'. To the subject in the now it seems perfectly self-evident what the present is: it is here and not there, and it is the now and not then. The past is behind us and the future lies ahead of us. In some ways, our reading of time has already informed us as subjects. But the experience of the uncanny should remind us that the now as a fulcrum for thinking about time is a lot less stable than we suppose. Henri Bergson suggests that the now is never stable, but is always in a state of becoming. Gilles Deleuze interrogates conventional temporal grammar, claiming that the 'past, present and future were not at all three parts of a single temporality, but that they rather formed two readings of time each of which is complete and excludes the other'.[46] In one reading, the present absorbs the past and the future into an eternal now or series of nows. In this reading the 'past and the future indicate only the relative difference between two presents'.[47] In the other reading, 'the present is nothing'. All that exists is the past and future into which the present is divided.[48] Bruno Latour goes further, uncoupling the traditional associations of linear temporality with teleology and progression, and destabilising the very concept of modernity on which the medieval depends.[49]

Yet despite the sophistication with which philosophers and critics have theorised time, modern or even classical notions of time prove remarkably durable.[50] As Dinshaw has suggested in her most recent book, 'the present moment is more temporally heterogeneous than academically disciplined, historically minded scholars tend to let on'.[51] So why does this conservative view of time persist? Part of the reason, as we will see, is institutional. Many medievalists are invested in a theory of time that requires what Dinshaw has characterised as professional time. Certain protocols define the professionals' approach to time. These protocols and the practices that surround them buttress institutional and professional identity. Dinshaw argues for the disruption of this identity and the theory of time in which it is implicated by looking outside the 'profession' to 'amateurs' who have a lot to tell us about the queer possibilities of time.

We would not disagree, but we are also aware that neither highly theoretical interventions nor a call to take non-professional thought seriously will be enough to move large groups of medievalists to change the way that they approach time and the past, While there are many medievalists who are not content with traditional approaches to history, there are many more who are disturbed to see the boundaries between medieval and its -ism, between past and present, becoming unstable (even if they do not express this view in public), just as there are many medievalists who are deeply concerned with historical accuracy in the way they portray, for example, the speech and customs of the Middle Ages.[52]

Sophisticated readers of medieval and medievalist texts may well admit that on an intellectual level time is a lot more complicated than it seems, but there's still something about more classical approaches to time that feels right. The past seems ... past, not easily touchable without subtle mediation. At the same time, many of these texts hold out hope that we can re-experience this past. Both feelings are in some sense fictional. We might be able to hold a medieval manuscript in our hands, but it is still only a fragment and a trace of the past. When we read about the creation of a machine that can travel through time, we experience the *frisson* of believing that it might be possible while also recognising its impossibility. This book is concerned with the dialectic between these two fictions. Our approach will often be affective and intuitive – largely based on how our feeling of time is elicited by medieval and medievalist texts. It is, in fact, part of our thesis that a number of these texts meditate on time precisely to implicate their readers in a theory or theories of time.[53] St Augustine was well aware that thinking about time could do strange things to a person: 'What then is time? Provided that no one asks me, I know. If I want to explain time to an inquirer, I do not know.'[54] Many of the fictions and practices of medievalism participate in the same paradox.

If medievalism is a kind of relationship to time, it can only be recollected in the doing of it. Medievalism is an action, or a practice, rather than a firm epistemological or ontological category and thus cannot be defined in opposition to, or the abjection of, what one might consider the 'really' medieval. In recent years, scholars such as John Ganim, Jeffrey Jerome Cohen, David Wallace and, of course, Carolyn Dinshaw have all made the case for understanding on a theoretical level what medievalism is in order to have an appreciation of the medieval, and it has been one of the founding principles of the journal *postmedieval: a journal of medieval cultural studies* (2010–) 'to develop a more present-minded medieval studies and a more historically-minded cultural studies'.[55] We too have made theoretical claims about the mutual imbrication of medieval studies and medievalism. Yet what links these different kinds of medievalism to the medieval remains contested. We need to cast our net wider. We need to capture not only epistemological and epistemic questions of periodisation, knowledge of the past and changing attitudes to the medieval. We also need to work with a lively sense of the changing disciplinary and institutional contexts of medieval studies, the various practices of medievalism inside and beyond the academy, and indeed the current state of the humanities. And we also need to capture the affective history of our disciplines: the love, the abjection and the discontent that variously frame our approaches to the medieval past, and to each other.

Feeling our way to the Middle Ages

Part of the issue, of course, is that it's difficult to know what we are connecting to. The Middle Ages suggests a transitional space rather than any coherent and well-defined period. It is tempting to call up the familiar claim – so attractive to a victim mentality – that the 'middleness' of the Middle Ages is simply a product of Renaissance humanism – an attempt to abject all of that which separates us from the wonders of the classical period. This runs the risk of buying into a host of categorical imperatives that abject and/or nostalgically recollect the medieval period. Collectively these imperatives reify divisions that are often more pragmatic than epistemological and gesture towards a view of history that is insistently whiggish, always and already leaving the past behind for a better future.[56] In ethical terms, this notion of progress privileges formations such as the modern state and secularised politics, leading us back into an abjection of all things medieval.[57] Medievalists of all stripes certainly know very well the dangers of indulging in the fantasy of a coherent period defined by being a 'middle', yet we continue to speak of the Middle Ages as if it actually existed, even though many would resist saying when and where it began and ended. Are we then, as Octavio Mannoni might suggest, simply indulging in a fetishistic disavowal that ultimately screens 'the way things really are'?[58] On one level we would say yes. Periodisation enables us to talk pragmatically about slices of history, but it also disables our capacity to see the connections between these different slices.

Does this mean that we should attempt to break through the ideological mist and show how the Middle Ages is really continuous with the periods that come before and after? We argue that this would be to misunderstand the nature of ideologically based periodisation. If the medieval is an ideological construction, then questions about when the Middle Ages ends, or whether it has ever

Introduction

ended, will enable us only 'to confirm our so-called "unconscious prejudices" with additional rationalizations'.[59]

At the same time, it is important to acknowledge that at the head of all the various ideologies that we will discuss in this volume lies the very idea of the boundary – the creation of time as space. To speak of the medieval, or of medievalism, even of neomedievalism, is to acknowledge this boundary. Thus, the discontent, or the unease, with which we approach the boundary of the Middle Ages is actually a symptom of the creation of the Middle Ages that is the perpetual practice of medievalism. To comprehend what we mean by the Middle Ages, we must understand the root of the unease with which we approach these boundaries, as they are erected, breached, ignored and erased. In a sense this is perfectly obvious to all those practitioners who have been examining things 'at the margins', and 'in the middle', but from another point of view the issue of boundaries has always seemed to be a problem, a constant nagging issue that seemingly detracts from our ability to visit the past, or to feel our way into medieval sensibilities.

In our first chapter we will consider the ways that the intertwined concepts of temporality and spatiality have produced the dominant compound idea of the Middle Ages as a place in time, apart from modernity and as if prior to medievalism. But temporal difference is also an affective issue, and throughout this book we will stress the various feelings and temperaments that affect the way we approach the Middle Ages.

Affective histories of the past are becoming increasingly common. The history of emotions is a burgeoning field of inquiry, and the field of medieval studies is no exception.[60] This is a field that encourages self-reflection, though it seems that the traditional impersonal rigour associated with medieval studies has inhibited most scholars from foregrounding their own emotional responses to the past. Such forays into the expression of personal feeling have not always met with approval, as we will show in chapter 4. But we argue that both medieval and medievalism studies are driven by powerful affective forces in their mutual relationships with each other and with the past they study. In particular, the chapters that follow work through the three emotions we name in our subtitle: love, abjection and discontent.

We have begun by invoking some of the different forms of love and desire for the past, and this will be a constant theme throughout: the way various writers, scholars and practitioners express their love and desire for the Middle Ages, its objects and its texts, and how those desires also shape the various practices of medievalism. But if we are often drawn to the *medium aevum*, it is just as common to abject and dismiss it, to rehearse a personal or cultural movement away from the medieval past. This push–pull dynamic of feeling has had a profound shaping force on medievalism, especially in the early modern period, but has also had a lasting effect on medieval studies and the vexed relationship between the two, leading to the third feeling on which we focus: discontent.

Discontent in medievalism can take many forms: discontent with one's own time or discontent with the limited ability to 'touch' another time; or indeed, with the indeterminacy between the literal and metaphorical aspects of such touching. These forms of discontents are often linked, and this is one of our guiding questions: what links the discontent of historical recovery with the discontent of imaginative recreation? And as we will show, there remains a large amount of disciplinary and institutional discontent on all sides of medieval and medievalist practice.

Our first chapter opens with a problem in medievalist texts that has hampered their attempts to connect with the past: that is, their tendency to be at once complicit in their abjection as merely medievalist, or secondary, texts and yet to insist on their magical ability to recuperate the past by actively investigating a past that remains unchanged and unknowing. This ambivalence at first seems to be limited to texts such as the clearly 'medievalist' *A Dream of John Ball* in which the protagonist can dreamily conjure up the past. It is most visible in the 'portal medievalism' we identify in works such as *The Lion, The Witch and the Wardrobe* that enable modern subjects to enter a fantasy of a 'medievalist' world. But in fact, these texts only enact and perhaps are generated by the medievalist phenomena that already exist in medieval texts themselves. *Sir Orfeo*, for instance, portrays its hero as entering into the magical land of faery in what might be seen as a very conventional iteration of the Otherworld narrative. At the same time, as a rewriting of the Orpheus story it references and is enfolded in a series of temporalities that marks it out as an action: a conscious medievalising of the medievals. The disciplinary relationship between the medieval and medievalist is put under pressure here by practices already at work within medieval literature and its textual and critical traditions.

In chapter 2 we turn to the question of the medieval 'real' and the manner in which the rejection of objective magic (initially voiced by Renaissance humanists) has tended to skew our understandings of medieval relics, influentially coding medieval 'belief' as simplistic and naive. We make the case that the feelings and beliefs brought on by these objects need to be taken seriously not only as a kind of post-medieval reception history of the object, but as a way in which the object attempts to communicate the past to us. As we think of medievalism as a form of practice, or action, rather than an ontological category, this leads us to the interpretation of material culture. Specifically, we look at how the properties of objects inevitably seem to bind us 'magically' to the past. This invocation of magic is generally met with a rationalistic recounting of the delusions brought on by such demented assertions. We take issue with these concerns about the 'inventions' (especially medieval) that accompany medieval objects such as relics, and conclude by making the case for an 'objective' history that is attentive to mood and affect.

Chapter 3 addresses the fear and abjection engendered by humanist approaches to history in the early modern period by diagnosing the fear generated by our attempts to recuperate the past as deriving not only from a fear of error but from a fear of death, as it was for the medievals. This death itself engenders fear because of its alien, unknowable nature, as becomes clear in the ritualistic invocation, 'timor mortis conturbat me' (the fear of death disturbs me). At the same time, the confusion that we feel in the face of death leads us to understand that this connects us with the past. Our attempts to control death via medievalist recreation, then, have the flavour of Freud's *fort-da* – a game that is as ancient as the Middle Ages itself as we encounter it in sources as various as Margery Kempe and William Dunbar.

In chapter 4, we examine the mechanism of affect as a potentially liberating way to 'touch' the Middle Ages. Specifically, we examine the ways in which affect in the post-medieval world engages and enables an understanding of the past. This chapter focuses primarily on the 'love' of Horace Walpole, the 'enthusiasm' of F. J. Furnivall and contemporary 'desirings' for the past. We make the case that this subjective understanding of the past need not be dismissed as inauthentic necromantic desire, or merely a narcissistic projection. Instead, it should be understood as a medium, that which makes possible our journey into the past: something, moreover, that was understood in the Middle Ages as a means by which the past could transmit itself to us.

In chapter 5 we offer some final speculations about the uncertain future of medieval and medievalism studies. We suggest that the general discontent this book diagnoses might well be seen as exemplary for many forms of historicist study within the humanities. Further, we suggest that attending to the connection between medieval and medievalist ideas about the university might well inform a postmodern response to the crisis in the humanities and the rapid corporatisation of higher education.

Notes

1. Pearsall, 'Interpretive models', p. 67.
2. Pearsall, 'Interpretive models', p. 67.
3. Specifically, he suggests that it might 'carry some impression of impropriety and indignity which enhances the image of the reversal of order' ('Interpretive models', p. 67).
4. Pearsall, 'Interpretive models', p. 67.
5. Pearsall, 'Interpretive models', p. 69.
6. Wolfe, *What Is Posthumanism?*, p. 106, quoted in Strohm, 'Historicity without historicism?', p. 382.
7. Strohm, 'Historicity without historicism?', pp. 381–2.
8. Burdick, *William Morris*, pp. 69–71.
9. Strohm, 'Historicity without historicism?', p. 387.
10. Ingham, 'Amorous dispossessions', p. 15.
11. Strohm, 'Historicity without historicism?', p. 387.
12. Ingham is responding to a claim made by Fradenburg in *Sacrifice Your Love*, pp. 44–5.
13. See, for instance, the work of Peter Sloterdijk as represented in Žižek, *The Sublime Object of Ideology*, p. 319.
14. Ingham, 'Amorous dispossessions', p. 20; Fradenburg, *Sacrifice Your Love*, p. 5.
15. Fradenburg, *Sacrifice Your Love*, p. 5.
16. Eco, 'Dreaming of the Middle Ages', p. 68.
17. Eco, 'Dreaming of the Middle Ages', p. 72.
18. www.themedievalacademyblog.org/medievalists-respond-to-charlottesville/, accessed 8 November 2017.
19. Eco, 'Dreaming of the Middle Ages', p. 71. This is also something that David Matthews seems to recognise, in *Medievalism*, p. 17. For further discussion, see the debate between Bruce Holsinger and Stephanie Trigg in *postmedieval*, 1:3 (2010).
20. The work of Carolyn Dinshaw in *How Soon Is Now?* is crucial here. We discuss this book in chapter 1. But for another perspective, see also Cramer, *Medieval Fantasy as Performance*. Cramer writes as both academic observer and participant in the Society for Creative Anachronism.
21. See for example, the overview of recent changing views of anachronism in Rouse, 'Rethinking anachronism'. A similar point is made by the editors of this volume in their introduction, p. 2.

Introduction

22 See for example, the work of Bildhauer, *Filming the Middle Ages* and Forni, *Chaucer's Afterlife*.
23 Furness, 'Hilary Mantel'.
24 Pugh and Weisl, *Medievalisms*. The book is 'a study of how the Middle Ages is continually reborn in subsequent centuries and of the persistent tropes that create this magical past' (p. 6).
25 Matthews, 'Chaucer's American accent', p. 759.
26 Emery and Utz (eds), *Medievalism*, p. 7.
27 The phrase is used memorably by Carolyn Dinshaw in *Getting Medieval*, passim.
28 Trigg, 'Once and future medievalism'.
29 Holsinger, 'Neomedievalism and international relations', p. 165. For further disambiguation of this term, see Lukes, 'Comparative neomedievalisms'.
30 Brown, 'Baphomet incorporated', p. 1.
31 Marshall, 'Neomedievalism', p. 24, quoting Robinson and Clements, 'Living with neomedievalism', p. 66.
32 See especially Helgeland's series of assertions that though he threw away much of his research into the Middle Ages in favour of artistic invention, the film was still 'medieval', in Prendergast and Trigg, 'The negative erotics of medievalism'.
33 In a recent issue of *postmedieval* devoted to the medievalism of nostalgia, Renée Trilling and Carolyn Dinshaw engage in a bit of give and take about the possibilities of nostalgia. Trilling takes a somewhat psychoanalytical view in arguing that nostalgic desire for the past and our disciplinary coding of the past as other set up a dialectic which refuses to choose between whether the 'medieval is truly past or always present' ('Medievalism and its discontents', p. 223). Dinshaw is more hopeful about nostalgia, calling for a 'critical nostalgia' in which the boundary between past and present is not nearly so well drawn as we might expect ('Nostalgia on my mind', p. 238). Though Trilling and Dinshaw disagree about the promise of nostalgia, and its relationship to temporality and temporal sequencing, they fundamentally agree about the centrality of nostalgia to medievalism.
34 Holsinger, *The Premodern Condition*; Cole and Smith (eds), *The Legitimacy of the Middle Ages*.
35 Dinshaw, *Getting Medieval*.
36 Tarantino (dir.), *Pulp Fiction*.
37 Tarantino (dir.), *Pulp Fiction*.
38 Dinshaw, *Getting Medieval*, p. 186.
39 That Dinshaw is aware that modern implements of torture and indeed the context itself is 'only' analogous becomes apparent a few pages later when she points out that 'the punishment for sodomy was castration for the first offense, death by fire for repeat offenders – rather like pliers and a blow torch' (*Getting Medieval*, p. 185).

40 Freud, *The Uncanny*, p. 148.
41 Bronfen, *Over Her Dead Body*, p. 113.
42 Trigg, 'Introduction', p. xix.
43 Our understanding of the medieval period via the gothic, as Chris Baldick has asserted, rests primarily on those eighteenth-century literary texts 'concerned with the brutality, cruelty, and superstition of the Middle Ages' (*The Oxford Book of Gothic Tales*, p. xii).
44 A quick look at some recent uses of the idea of the *Unheimlich* by medievalists might include Cohen, *Of Giants*, pp. 25, 145; Fradenburg, *Sacrifice Your Love*, p. 70; Prendergast, *Chaucer's Dead Body*, pp. 71–84.
45 Smith, *Arts of Possession*, p. 44.
46 Deleuze, *The Logic of Sense*, p. 72.
47 Deleuze, *The Logic of Sense*, p. 73.
48 Deleuze, *The Logic of Sense*, p. 73.
49 Latour, *We Have Never Been Modern*, p. 47.
50 As Dinshaw points out, Michel Serres characterises linear, measurably constant time as 'classical time' (*How Soon Is Now?*, p. 8).
51 Dinshaw, *How Soon Is Now?*, p. xiv.
52 See, for example, the essays by fiction writers Robyn Cadwallader, Gillian Polack and Eric Jager in the special issue of *postmedieval* on historical fiction, *postmedieval* 7:2 (2016).
53 Theoreticians of time have routinely used fictions to lead their audiences to think through time. The most obvious example is Friedrich Nietzsche's meditation on the eternal return in *Also sprach Zarathustra*, but contemporary philosophers such as Bernard Stiegler have seen fiction (or in his case myth) as more than illustrative – as instantiations of historical understandings of temporality that resonate in the here and now (*Technics and Time*). Henri Bergson, in fact, constructed his work *Matière et mémoire* as a fiction, saying that when we read his work we have to pretend (*feindre*) that we have no preconceptions of the real, the ideal, matter and spirit in order to experience the idea of time in which he wishes to immerse us (p. 11). The idea was to replace so-called pure and objective approaches to temporality that purportedly stood outside of time with experiential understandings of time within time. See Alipaz, 'Merleau-Ponty's Bergson', pp. 66–83. And for a more autobiographical discussion of the 'time' of the medieval scholar working with a disability, see Godden, 'Getting medieval in real time', pp. 267–77.
54 Augustine, *Confessions*, p. 230.
55 This aim appears with minor variations on the frontispiece of the journal, as the mission statement of the BABEL working group that edits the journal.
56 Compare Patterson in *Negotiating the Past*.
57 Davis, 'The sense of an epoch', pp. 39–69.

58 Mannoni, 'I know well', pp. 68–92.
59 Žižek, *The Sublime Object of Ideology*, p. 48. For a recent assertion about how 'we have always been medieval', see Cole and Smith (eds), 'Introduction: outside modernity', *The Legitimacy of the Middle Ages*, p. 24.
60 Key texts for the history of medieval emotions include Rosenwein, *Anger's Past*, *Emotional Communities* and *Generations of Feeling*; McNamer, *Affective Meditation and the Invention of Medieval Compassion*; Nagy and Bouquet, *Sensible Moyen Age*; and Downes and McNamara, 'The history of emotions and Middle English literature'. For medievalism, see Utz, *Medievalism: A Manifesto*, pp. 3–4.

1
The space of time and the medievalist imaginary

> Did it start with Bergson, or before? Space was treated as the dead, the fixed, the undialectical, the immobile. Time, on the contrary, was richness, fecundity, life, dialectic.
>
> Michel Foucault[1]

The traditional ontology of the medieval is a familiar story, grounded on the simple historical progression from the medieval as the primary text or object of study, to the post-medieval, understood as anything in the form of commentary, reception or invention. The Middle Ages come to an end, and then at various points in time it becomes desirable to invoke, abject, re-invent, and study them from the post-medieval present. This chronological ordering of the difference between the medieval and modern – and the ontological and epistemological priority of the medieval it seems to guarantee – is the 'common-sense' view.[2] As Mike Rodman Jones comments, 'For medievalism of any kind to exist, the Middle Ages need to be over.'[3] Until relatively recently, this straightforward and eminently reasonable narrative was foundational to a range of disciplines and practices. This held true for medieval historians and historicist literary critics trying to get back to the historical past and free it from modern preconceptions, as well as practitioners of medievalism asserting their right to reconstruct the Middle Ages using methods that might well be scholarly, but that might equally be more creative and inventive. No matter what the social, intellectual, personal or political desires these reconstructions enact, in this ontological hierarchy, the medieval, as the temporally prior period, takes epistemological precedence over the post-medieval as its primary reference point.

This hierarchy takes a number of different forms, some of which we will visit over the course of this book. This first chapter works through some of the corollaries of this implicit understanding of the medieval as stable and finite, and the medievalist as structured by change, mobility, interpretative variety and ideological work.[4] When the medieval era is characterised by stability and fixity, there is an easy slippage from temporal to spatial finitude: the medieval thus becomes a place one might 'visit' and inhabit. We will argue that this view of the medieval is convenient and enabling for both medieval studies and medievalist practice, since it cedes the intellectual challenges and pleasures of hermeneutic discovery, methodological experiment and imaginative play entirely to the present. Such stability is not dissimilar to the familiar idea of the Middle Ages as hegemonic and unchanging, bound throughout, from beginning to end, by conservative, feudal ideology – an idea that has rightly come under substantial critique, as we will see later; but at this point we focus on the frequency with which temporal and cultural difference is conceived as spatial otherness, and how influential this conception of the Middle Ages has been. When modernity thinks about visiting the past, the Middle Ages is its most common destination.

Our agenda is larger than a critique of too rigid an opposition between the medieval and the modern, though it certainly has many affinities with the work of other scholars working in that vein.[5] Throughout this book, we seek to re-figure the customary, but rather more slippery distinction between the medieval and the medievalist.[6] Despite appearances to the contrary, the latter is rarely only or simply a derivative, imitative replica of a pristine historical past. Instead, we suggest these two formations have always been constitutive, though unevenly, of each other; and that contrary to the narratives offered by traditional disciplinary histories of medieval studies and medievalism, neither can truly claim a stable ontological priority over the other.

While we might expect the academic discipline of medieval studies to bolster the priority of the historical Middle Ages, as it mostly does, it is one of the great paradoxes of medievalism that many of its own fictions also promote this simplified reading of their own genesis and dependence on medieval origins. In spite of the spirit of play and creative invention we customarily associate with medievalism, many of its practitioners persistently appeal, either explicitly or implicitly, to the ontological stability and priority of the Middle Ages. This is especially the case in those medievalist stories that are predicated on the possibility of temporal movement between the modern era and the medieval past; or that rely on the differences in affective or emotional responses between medieval and modern people. In such fictions of cultural transmission, the starkness of the opposition between the medieval and the post-medieval is especially noticeable.

Portal medievalism: Travelling to the past

Medievalist time-travel narratives depend on a clear opposition between the medieval and its other as they traverse linear movements backwards and forwards. But the possibility of movement between the two eras is usually seen as a distinctive property of the medievalist alone, powered by a modern imagination that is able to observe and describe without limits both the medieval and its afterlife, as opposed to the medieval past which cannot see its own future. If the medieval imaginary, to use Nickolas Haydock's term,[7] refers to the characteristic features of the Middle Ages, as represented in medieval film, we might coin a parallel phrase: the medievalist imaginary. This would refer to medievalism's dual insistence that it is both derivative and recuperative. In this logic, medievalism appears secondary to the medieval, but in its very promise to ease our path 'back' to the Middle Ages, medievalism demonstrates its mastery over both the old and the new through its capacity to move between them. Medievalism thus masks its mutually constitutive *conceptual* relationship with the medieval by presenting itself as the active remaker, reinventor and recreator of the Middle Ages, empowered with the imagination and the technology to take us there.

This conceptual relationship is often eased, but attractively blurred, or obscured, by material culture. In a modernity enchanted by its own past, medieval objects – relics, stones, textiles, manuscripts, jewels, buildings and built spaces – regularly carry the touch of the medieval real into the modern world. Such objects and places seem to help us experience the medieval past, whether we are acting as consumers, tourists or scholars. These 'real' medieval objects are accorded a strong affective charge that is akin to a kind of secular magic; and this affective relationship is sustained by the idea that the medieval is a stable place to which one can turn and return. Kathleen Davis and Nadia Altschul rightly insist that the conceptual histories of the Middle Ages and Europe have been 'mutually constitutive'. They are both part of a 'temporal grid' and a 'spatial imaginary' that supplies a 'spatiotemporal baseline for many dominant narratives'.[8] This 'baseline' bolsters the familiar presupposition that it might be enough to stand or walk in a space where medieval people lived and moved (for example, a church, a city wall, a pilgrimage site) to bring you 'closer' to the medieval past.[9] This is a foundational premise not only of cultural and heritage tourism but also of the idea that scholars living outside Europe will have to work harder to truly 'understand' the medieval past. While such a thinly veiled colonialism is expressed more often informally than in print, it is one that many non-European scholars will recognise. Thus, although postmodern geography has only recently returned our attention to space, space has in many senses determined how the Middle Ages was thought to have existed for quite some time.[10] This conception of the past was, as Foucault suggests, a space that was fixed and immobile – and dead in the sense that it provided satisfaction, an endpoint to the desire to know.

This desire for the past is often fed by the possibility of travelling back in time, as if to another country or region. We suggest, indeed, that the medieval past is one of the most popular destinations of such travel, because of its customary alterity from modernity. This has been a particular feature of medievalist cinema and its delight in the visual and scenic otherness of the medieval past: at once instantly recognisable but lovingly presented as exotic and strange. The medieval past is often posited as significant for modernity but satisfyingly distant from it: when time-travel fictions open up the possibility of travelling to the past, the Middle Ages are one of the most frequent destinations.

In one of the earliest and most famous imaginings of time travel, for example, H. G. Wells's *The Time Machine* (1895), the possibility of temporal movement through a 'scientific' invention leads almost immediately to the possibility of travel to the Middle Ages:

> 'It would be remarkably convenient for the historian,' the Psychologist suggested. 'One might travel back and verify the accepted account of the Battle of Hastings, for instance!'
> 'Don't you think you would attract attention?' said the Medical Man. 'Our ancestors had no great tolerance for anachronisms.'[11]

This remark certainly suggests a form of historicism that relies on a technological fantasy – if it could only be built, a machine could objectively go to an already existing stable place (as well as time) and discover, for instance, whether King Harold *really was* shot in the eye with an arrow. And, in this way, a foundational national narrative could be corrected and firmed up. But as with so many time-travel narratives it almost immediately becomes apparent that once the boundary of the closed-off temporal space is transgressed, that transgression threatens to undo the stability of the period. In fact, it is the very intolerance of 'anachronism' – a kind of foundational stability – that is threatened here by the very person who has gone to observe and confirm stability. Wells's fantasy configures the Middle Ages as the exemplary closed, inviolate space of the past. In other words, we might start to understand them, but they could never understand us. This is a persistent and enabling fiction that both enables the work of traditional medieval studies and licenses the imaginative project of medievalism.

As many commentators and historians have shown, the nineteenth century was a crucial period for the passionate study of the Middle Ages and the medievalist desire to return there.[12] From the 1840s, in particular, the medievalist imaginary gathers strength at a time when the cultural and social contrast between the medieval world and the rapidly changing industrialised West was experienced as particularly acute, when the scholarly study of medieval literature was also flourishing. Older forms of medievalism in the Gothic eighteenth century might have constructed fake medieval or gothic follies,[13] and Renaissance and Restoration collectors might have treasured real survivals from the medieval past, as we will show in chapter 2, but in this later period the desire to *transport* the modern subject into the medieval past, or a reformed medievalist future, took more concrete form in creative fictions that would set the agenda for the next century's prolific medievalism.[14]

Three influential texts, published within two years of each other, by William Morris and Mark Twain, share a fascination with the contrast and juxtaposition between medieval and modern subjectivities, as well as the possibility of moving backwards, and forwards, in time, even as they seem to come from very different ideological positions, and offer very different though equally influential representations of the medieval past.[15] Morris's *A Dream of John Ball* (1888) and *News from Nowhere* (1890) both offer medievalist visionary narratives: the first a dream back to the medieval past; the second a futuristic neo-medievalism. The narrator of *A Dream of John Ball* says he regularly dreams, when asleep, of medieval architectural sites such as churches and villages, though they are often admixed with the new. In this text, the movement between medieval times and the present is not traumatic, but restful and easy:

> Sometimes I am rewarded for fretting myself so much about present matters by a quite unasked-for pleasant dream. I mean when

> I am asleep. This dream is as it were a present of an architectural peep-show. I see some beautiful and noble building new made, as it were for the occasion, as clearly as if I were awake; not vaguely or absurdly, as often happens in dreams, but with all the detail clear and reasonable. Some Elizabethan house with its scrap of earlier fourteenth-century building, and its later degradations of Queen Anne and Silly Billy and Victoria, marring but not destroying it, in an old village once a clearing amid the sandy woodlands of Sussex.
>
> ...
>
> All this I have seen in the dreams of the night clearer than I can force myself to see them in dreams of the day. So that it would have been nothing new to me the other night to fall into an architectural dream if that were all, and yet I have to tell of things strange and new that befell me after I had fallen asleep.[16]

As we might expect from Morris, there is a keen interest in domestic interiors and the capacity of the 'architectural dream' in *A Dream of John Ball*: the first time the dreamer enters the house in his dream, the room he finds is 'strange and beautiful' and the decorative interior is rough but bright and free. The sideboard is 'quaintly-carved', the pewter is 'bright', the carved oak furniture is 'stout' and 'rough':

> The walls were panelled roughly enough with oak boards to about six feet from the floor, and about three feet of plaster above that was wrought in a pattern of a rose stem running all round the room, freely and roughly done, but with (as it seemed to my unused eyes) wonderful skill and spirit.[17]

Here is nineteenth-century domestic medievalism – also available, incidentally, for purchase in the products and designs of Morris and Company – in its 'natural' environment.[18] The journey is not only temporal but spatial as the dreamer travels, like a Chaucerian dream-narrator, from his London room in the late nineteenth century to fourteenth-century Kent. The relationship with the past here is literally dialogic, since much of the work is concerned with a conversation that the protagonist has with the Lollard priest John Ball. As the protagonist puts it, 'so we sat, and I gathered my thoughts to hear what he would say, and I myself was trying to think what I should ask of him; for I thought of him as he of me, that he had seen things which I could not have seen'.[19] But, as with any number of medievalist imaginaries, the fantasy is that the interaction with the past will not alter it. John Ball, as the protagonist tells him, will die and the Rising of 1381 'shall come to nought by seeming'.[20] All that was for the protagonist will be for John Ball.

Similarly, in *News from Nowhere*, a young man, engaged in revolutionary activity, travels home after a meeting, disgruntled with its failure to show a path to a reformed future in the midst of a gritty, grimy, industrial present: 'in that vapour-bath of hurried and discontented humanity, a carriage of the underground railway, he, like others, stewed discontentedly'.[21] But emerging from the station at Hammersmith, he is refreshed by a soft breeze across the river in the moonlight, and falls dreamily asleep. When he wakes, it is summer and it gradually becomes clear that he has slept through into a vision of a future, more equitable society that is a mixture of old and new, medieval and futuristic. It collapses time and space, as it is set in a future London, where the Houses of Parliament have become a kind of dung market. The defamiliarisation of modernity is relentless, as one character tells the dreamer, 'my old kinsman has given me books to read about the strange game they played there'.[22] But the accounts of the past are not always correct or, when they are correct, are figured to be 'a rotten collection of lies' and it falls to the man from the past to correct the future.[23] The past (here the 'present') is unchanging and there is a strange sense that the future may be unchanging as well, as the dreamer says that what he saw was not a dream but a vision in which he understands one character to have said, 'go back again, now you have seen us, and your outward eyes have learned that in spite of all the infallible maxims of your day there is yet a time of rest in store for the world'.[24]

Morris's utopic vision might seem to sit uneasily with his earlier dream of John Ball. As Patricia Ingham suggests, utopia is seen as 'shot through with the sheen of the new; the medieval, on the other hand, rarely associated with innovation or an active avant garde, seems thus unused, if not unable, to conjure the utopian'.[25] Yet Morris makes claims for an analogical historical progression that brings past, present and future together. The ability to 'dream' the past is 'nothing new', yet it can give rise to things 'strange and new'. The future defamiliarises the present, but in familiar terms. In formal terms, Morris's fictions are resolutely dialogic, but nonetheless resolve themselves into some certain epistemic formation that reflected the 'result of a historical logic that was cunning, if indirect' – 'moving forward ever towards something that seems the opposite of that which it started from, and yet the earlier order never dead but living in the new, and slowly moulding it to a recreation of its former self'.[26]

Side by side with this unchanging view of time seems to be its opposite, a narrative in which the protagonist travels back in time only to bring his own dystopic modernity with him. In contrast to the dreamy and easy transitions in Morris's works, the time-travel mechanism in Mark Twain's *A Connecticut Yankee at King Arthur's Court* (1889) is straightforwardly traumatic: a nasty blow on the head, and the hero finds himself in medieval Camelot, where he immediately sets out to modernise, to transform and reform its feudalism, and to inject some confident industrialisation and technology into a society coded decisively, even derisively, as backward. His actions seem to have a dramatic and lasting effect on the past as the novel ends with the slaughter of twenty-five thousand knights by a Gatling gun, but, crucially, history fails to record the traumatic events. It remains unclear if we are to take it as a fiction that relies on a medievalist 'delirium' that clouds the Yankee's mind, or as a fiction that depends on a medieval imaginary.

All three novels are some of the earliest, dramatic and most influential examples of a phenomenon we call 'portal medievalism': fictions that foreground the mode of entry into (or out of) medieval space and time. Where medievalist fantasies such as *The Lord of the Rings* or *Game of Thrones* present worlds whose medievalist mise-en-scène is utterly self-contained, portal medievalism is structured more literally around the transition from one world to another, whether in an elaborate time machine, through the back of a wardrobe, a blow on the head or some other visionary or technological means. This is where medievalism often meets science fiction. Doctor Who, for example, travelled in his TARDIS to the Middle Ages on a number of occasions.[27] Sometimes, the mechanisms for moving backward in time draw on the conceptual architecture and technologies of contemporary science, like the machines that use quantum and particle theory to 'travel' (dismantle and reassemble the body) to simultaneous multiple worlds (and specifically, fourteenth-century France) in Michael Crichton's *Timeline* (2000). Sometimes they are more vaguely futuristic, like the late twenty-first-century 'time travel net' that sends Oxford researchers back to the past in Connie Willis's *Doomsday Book* (1992). This last example incidentally implies that the historical research of the future will *still* not know enough about the fourteenth century: the best 'academic' training in linguistics and sociology still leaves the hapless time traveller almost completely at a loss when faced with the 'real' Middle Ages. But whatever the means of entry, the idea of the portal is particularly compelling because it literalises and concretises the otherness of the Middle Ages, as a place we can literally walk into. Passing through a portal of some kind also suggests subconsciously that this other world represents a different psychic or mental state of our own unconscious (here the affinities of medievalism with the gothic are most profound); or that we ourselves might be changed as we enter this other world.[28]

It is crucial that these portals are difficult or unyielding in some way. In both of Morris's works, it is clear that the protagonists have been granted a vision of the past/future but will be unable to return to it. And Twain's time traveller has supposedly slept for eight hundred years and will only be reunited with his (medieval) beloved in death. Reminiscent of medieval journeys to the Otherworld, or the search for the Grail castle, the conditions for passing through the portal are not always consistent, or easily replicated. The medievalist imaginary is predicated on the difficulty of passing between worlds: it can never be given to everyone, not all the time. Medievalist time-travel romances and children's fiction, for example, regularly feature talismanic objects (a ring, a jewel, a book) that have lain neglected or unrecognised for centuries until the right person appears who can harness or benefit from their powers.[29]

Not all medievalist fictions deploy portal medievalism, of course, but we are particularly concerned with such movement in and out of the medieval world, because it helps us to show how the processes of historical reconstruction, the structures of periodisation and the creative work of medievalism are all intricately, and suggestively, bound to ideas of space as much as the idea of temporal dislocation. The possibility of leaving the medieval behind is what constitutes the medieval in the first place. But however much the past and the present seem to be distinguished, there is always a kind of temporal leakage.[30] In Morris's *A Dream of John Ball*, the protagonist distinguishes his dream from the normal 'architectural dream' by relating things of the past that are yet 'strange and new'. The dreamer of *News from Nowhere* characterises the future as the past, saying the houses were 'so like mediæval houses of the same materials that I fairly felt as if I were alive in the fourteenth century'.[31]

In the case of Twain, there is a manuscript (of which the novel is a transcription): 'parchment, and yellow with age … a palimpsest. Under the old dim writing of the Yankee historian appeared traces of a penmanship which was older and dimmer still – Latin words and sentences: fragments from old monkish legends, evidently.'[32] Modernity here literally overwrites the Middle Ages, but this medieval modernity is rejected as impossible. Even evidence of a bullet

The space of time and the medievalist imaginary

hole in the armour of a knight is dismissed by a nineteenth-century museum guide as a malicious action by Cromwell's soldiers.

Portal medievalism is just one aspect of medievalist time travel, a capacious category that is a feature of much medievalist fiction and especially film, a medium that delights in the visual contrast between medieval and modern. These contrasts, and the ideological and imaginative work they perform, have been much discussed by scholars. In some key examples, Nickolas Haydock offers a Deleuzian reading of the 'time-image' in medievalist cinema; Louise D'Arcens considers the phenomenon of 'temporal compression' and the performance of tradition across different temporalities of medievalism; and Bettina Bildhauer analyses 'non-linear' time in cinematic medievalism, especially Friedric Willhelm Murnau's *Faust* and Fritz Lang's *Destiny*, in *Filming the Middle Ages*.[33]

This form of medievalism often enacts a kind of fantasy about time that reorients the way we relate to it; in part by implicitly claiming that the capacity to manipulate time is a modern property, with curiosity about the medieval past as the driving motivation. In the remainder of this chapter, however, we would like to explore the extent to which medieval notions of space and time themselves are partly constitutive of medievalist projects of temporal space.

Layered temporalities and temporal allegories

Our focus on the self-conscious medievalist inventions of the nineteenth century and the popularity of time travel in twentieth- and twenty-first-century film and fiction might seem to identify popular suspicions about the closed, fixed and supersessional nature of time as a creation of medievalism. But nothing could be farther from the truth. Medieval literature is itself regularly engaged by the possibilities of temporal switching, or the suspension of time. Similarly, medieval writers are often equally conscious of the cultural layering that facilitates the imaginative movement between understandings of cosmological, seasonal, sacred and mercantile time.

In medieval imaginative fictions, our chief concern in this section, different times and places are regularly mapped onto one another. Indeed, this form of cultural synthesis is a common property of medieval literature, and familiar examples abound. We think of the fourteenth-century court culture of Troy in Chaucer's *Troilus and Criseyde* or the layering of Athenian, Theban and Boethian culture in *The Knight's Tale*; the very English re-staging of the Crucifixion in *Piers Plowman*, or the playful Christian anachronisms of the mystery plays. The habits of exegetical thought — reading anagogically — meant that the possibility of another temporality was ever-present. In the celebrated argument of Margery Kempe, answering the priest who challenges her deeply felt and tearful response to the idea of the Crucifixion, so too ought the image of Christ on the cross be with us always.[34] In contrast to modernity's image of the Middle Ages as tightly sealed and homogeneous, immune from change and difference, medieval literature often works with a temporal understanding that is quite porous and flexible.

This temporal flexibility has been criticised as a conceptual weakness of medieval culture, especially when it is judged in relation to modern historiographic conventions of linear time and causality.[35] Indeed, we are tempted to suggest it may be that one of the (perverse) reasons modernity has insisted so strongly that the Middle Ages names a finite period is precisely because medieval culture consistently demonstrates an awareness of its own much more complex sense that temporalities are layered, overlapping and porous. Medieval people may not have been conscious of themselves as 'in the middle', between the two more sophisticated epistemes of antiquity and modernity, but medieval culture at least does often bear witness to this sense that temporalities are not always finite and enclosed; that time can be measured in different ways; and that what Michel Serres has characterised in both temporal and topological terms as temporal pleating — the juxtapositioning of two time zones — is rich material for narrative.[36] Bruno Latour similarly emphasises the spiral — as opposed to the linear — movement of temporality, and the challenge this offers to modernity.[37] Dipesh Chakrabarty, among others, reminds us that Western conceptions of time are often layered, and complicated, blending colonial and postcolonial understandings of time, duration and cultural understanding. Many contemporary theories of time are focused on the making and measuring of modernity and, in this regard, they have deep implications for our understanding of medieval time, especially when the past is conceived in spatial terms.[38] A common theme amongst medieval scholars such as Jeffrey Jerome Cohen and Paul Strohm, who engage most closely with temporality theory, is the disruption of 'the Middle Ages' as temporally bounded and discrete, as we have argued above.[39]

Most cogently, however, in her recent study, *How Soon Is Now?*, Carolyn Dinshaw explores the idea of a thick, multiple present which she labels 'temporal heterogeneity' in a rich array of medieval and some medievalist texts. In Dinshaw's thesis, such asynchrony is associated with a form of queer, unreproductive, non-normative sexuality she links to her history of 'amateur' medievalism. Dinshaw develops this model in her first chapter through a series of stories about individuals – all male – who, through some kind of divine intervention, step out of the stream of time for a long period. These stories of asynchrony, like the *Northern Homily* story of the monk and the bird that becomes exemplary in her chapter, are about temporal shifts and movements of individuals across time; individuals who sleep for long periods – up to three hundred years – while quotidian time passes by, as the people they knew die, and as the seasons and years pass on without them. The world into which they wake is marked by an uncanny similarity to the one in which they fell asleep, except that they are unrecognisable (and not just for their long beards) to everyone, and recognise no one. Time has passed, and individuals and family members have died, though social and cultural structures usually remain stable: these medieval stories of shifting temporalities mostly foreground the psychological trauma or spiritual revelation that results from this dramatic break in an individual's relationship to society. They are classical and medieval stories about asynchrony, then, but the stories are personal and individual in effect, tending not to foreground cultural or social switching between periods or epistemic formations.

The major exception, as Dinshaw notes, is the fable of the Seven Sleepers of Ephesus, made popular by Jacobus de Voragine. In this story, seven Christians avoid persecution for their beliefs by retreating from Rome in the reign of the emperor Decius. They take refuge in a cave where they sleep, miraculously preserved, for 362 years. When they wake, it is thirty years into the reign of Theodosius, who had been baptised in 380. They thus emerge into a Christian era, and their long sleep is interpreted as divine intervention. The Sleepers are then able to help Theodosius in his battle against heretics who deny the resurrection of the dead.[40]

One of Dinshaw's chief concerns in this story is with its interest in asynchrony and the possibility that it may be embodied, constitutive of being human, or, as she writes, 'in our bones'.[41] One of the sleepers, Maximian, explains that the seven were in the cave as a child rests, without fear or harm, in the mother's womb: 'Truly moreover we are resurrected and live, and like an infant in the womb of a mother feels no harm and lives so we were living and lying and sleeping and not feeling.'

(Vere enim resurreximus et vivimus, et sicut infans est in utero matris non sentiens laesionem et vivit, sic fuimus viventes, iacentes et dormientes et non sentientes.)[42] In this analogy, the baby is perceived as if fully formed, but protected 'from harm, from even the harms of time', while waiting to be born, when 'the mother with the atemporal in her gives life, and is associated with even more life: resurrection'.[43] Dinshaw argues that this analogy 'brings asynchrony firmly into the realm of the everyday and of everyone', not just the exceptional seven sleepers: 'While offering a most vivid example of extraordinary temporal multiplicity, this saint's life also suggests that *everyone* began life in a nine months' sleep.'[44] She returns to this argument later in the book, as it is part of her general thesis that if 'we all began life asynchronously ... this experience provides us all with the ground for feeling that other temporalities press upon mundanely sequential chronologies'.[45]

Dinshaw's extension of Maximian's analogy is not unproblematic, however. His comparison between several centuries of sleep and a nine-month gestation seems persuasive enough in philosophical or allegorical terms: the womb-like cave protects the sleepers from physical, emotional and temporal damage, while time passes outside and the conditions for religious persecution abate. But the story and the analogy have a peculiar relationship. As Dinshaw notes, the sleepers are awakened in order to demonstrate the doctrine of the resurrection of the body. Yet the sleepers were not resurrected from the dead (despite the fact that Theodosius compares them to Lazarus). The relationship between the reawakening and the rationale for the reawakening works at an analogical level much like the relationship between the sleepers and the child. This analogy actually suggests something other than stasis. Contemporary beliefs might well code early understandings of the womb as quiescent, but medieval notions of this space were completely implicated in temporality. The womb is *outside* time, but marks the passage of time, as the foetus grows. This was certainly a medieval view. The medieval *Trotula* text, for instance, shows how the foetus is thought of as quite actively changing and growing according to a strict nine-month schedule:

> In the first month, there is purgation of the blood. In the second month, there is expression of the blood and the body. In the third month, [the foetus] produces nails and hair. In the fourth month,

it begins to move and for the ninth month, it proceeds from the darkness into the light.⁴⁶

Time is not suspended here as it might be in sleep, but decisively measures the stages of the growing body. The foetus progresses firmly and positively through its regular stages of change and development, and with the direct intervention of Nature, moves inexorably 'into the light'. So why invoke as *beyond time* a space that is so deeply implicated in the temporal? Our belief is that far from being conceived of as a timeless space, the womb analogy was meant to convey the *passage of time* within the cave. The miracle of the sleepers, then, is that time passes for them while they sleep, but they do not die (something that seems to be clear when, just after Maximian makes his analogy, the narrator tells us that '[the sleepers] inclined their heads to the earth, and rendered their spirits at the command of our Lord Jesus Christ, and so died').⁴⁷ Space here is implicated in time and time in space. The geographer Doreen Massey might almost be speaking of the medieval story when she says, 'What you will find here is an attempt to awaken space by the long sleep engendered by the inattention of the past.'⁴⁸ The cave, like the sleepers' bodies, remains within time even if hidden from view.

We labour this point because Dinshaw draws heavily on Maximian's account of his experience to extrapolate a more general theory about the everyday, and universal asynchrony. While we agree that medieval temporalities are often creatively fluid, porous and open-ended, Dinshaw strains, we think, to argue that asynchrony is universal and ahistorical when she argues 'that *everyone* began life in a nine months' sleep'; and suggests that we may all have asynchrony 'in our bones' because the mother has "the atemporal in her."⁴⁹ In contrast, we argue that space might well be asynchronous but it is never atemporal. And bodies as extended in space (and as spaces themselves) are always implicated in time though they too can be out of joint. And despite our desire to thicken the relationships between the medieval and the medievalist, we would not go so far as to suggest that they are co-extensive, that we all experience them, and time, in the same universal way.

This issue (and some of our own back-and-forth dialogues at conferences and in conversations with Carolyn Dinshaw over the last ten years) is for us one of the most productive and intriguing aspects of the discussion about multiple temporalities and asynchrony: the play of difference over whether such experiences are indeed normative or exceptional and miraculous, like a portal that will open only to a select few. This is a particularly productive dialectic for medievalism, for as we have started to show, medievalist fictions themselves have it both ways. Access to the medieval past is both easy and difficult. Writers and readers of medievalist texts take for granted that imagining travel to the past is both comprehensible and familiar (time travel is barely a controversial fictional strategy); but the actual experience itself is always exceptional and difficult for the characters who must negotiate those borders. We need to keep all these variants and possibilities in mind as we compare and contrast medieval and medievalist techniques of crossing temporalities.

Our interest in medievalist temporality narratives, then, is complementary with Dinshaw's, but oriented in a different direction. Many of her exemplary narratives, like that of the Seven Sleepers, are about what happens when time seems to slip by without our noticing, when individual subjects like Rip Van Winkle find themselves dislocated from their original time zone. Alternatively, as in Dinshaw's layered and nuanced account of Margery Kempe, Hope Emily Allen and her relationship with the medieval mystic and her own scholarly predecessor at Bryn Mawr, individuals become conscious of experiencing multiple temporalities through relationships across time with other individuals, texts or objects. Our concern, by contrast, is with larger patterns of medieval and medievalist temporal switching: the capacity to register and map cultural and political change across eras.

We turn now to consider some medieval texts that display a consciousness of the temporal and cultural boundaries of the Middle Ages. We do not mean simply the passing of historical time or the consciousness of different temporal modalities that can be sustained simultaneously by a given society (for example, linear, cyclic or eschatological time),[50] but an awareness that temporal progression can bring about epistemic and cultural change. Awareness of such difference is a rich resource for imaginative and creative fictions, and we argue that such awareness is in part constitutive of the Middle Ages. This is a very different image from the self-enclosed and myopic 'middle' or 'dark' ages conceived by early modern writers rushing quickly past these centuries on their way to recuperate a classical past. We are interested here in a Middle Ages that can see differences within itself, and that can also conceive of eras other than itself, often in quite passionate and emotional ways. This consciousness of cultural alterity is also generative of

The space of time and the medievalist imaginary

medievalism, as a cultural practice that is driven by the play of difference and similarity between the medieval and the post-medieval. These medieval texts, then, do not simply register the passing of time, or the effect of weird temporalities on individual subjects; they actively manipulate time, working in spaces to imagine alternative national and urban histories.

The space of English time

We turn now to three medieval texts that seem to treat the 'pre-medieval' past very differently, but in fact enact a temporal logic that is recognisable as what we think of as medievalism. It is, of course, unremarkable that many of these texts tend to have Christian valences. As Renée R. Trilling argues, one of the dominant modes of historiography, especially in the early Middle Ages, imagined time 'as a narrative of salvation in which time was a progression toward a Day of Judgment, with well-defined boundaries between past and present and a clearly articulated telos of meaning'.[51] Such texts not only gave shape to the past, but provided a model for understanding the present – particularly when that present seemed not to fit into such a clear telos.

The earliest example of this kind of universal salvational history being explicitly tied to the more localised history of England is Gildas's sixth-century *De Excidio et Conquestu Britanniae*. In what Robert W. Hanning has termed 'the fall of Britain tradition', Gildas reveals himself to be one of the earliest discontents of medieval history and civilisation: his national history is an avowedly emotional and affective one:[52]

> What I have to deplore with mournful complaint is a general loss of good, a heaping of bad. But ... I sympathize with my country's difficulties and troubles, and rejoice in remedies to relieve them. I [have] decided to speak of the dangers run not by soldiers in the stress of war but by the lazy.[53]

Gildas's lament and the history that will follow are both preludes to part three of his letter, an exhortation that is framed in biblical terms. Complaining about current bad times is a feature of much historical and political writing, of course, while Gildas adds a more long-term complaint about the laziness and sloth of the Britons. This is not the nostalgic medievalism of a Malory, mourning the passing of an older, better culture; nor any version of lament for an older heroic mode. Instead, Gildas positions himself firmly in opposition to heroic culture.[54] His history is one of progressive waves of colonisation in Britain: the arrival of the Romans and their subsequent neglect of the country. At the same time, he evokes the national culture of 'this island, stiff-necked and haughty'.[55] The island's history is a deeply political one, but it is also a mixed religious history. The landscape, once animated with malevolent spirits, is marked with 'devilish monstrosities', and their gothic 'outlines still ugly, faces still grim':

> I shall not speak of the ancient errors, common to all races, that bound the whole of humanity fast before the coming of Christ in the flesh. I shall not enumerate the devilish monstrosities of my land, numerous, almost as those that plagued Egypt, some of which we can see today, stark as ever, inside or outside deserted city wall: outlines still ugly, faces still grim. I shall not name the mountains and hills and rivers, once so pernicious, now useful for human needs, on which, in those days, a blind people heaped honors.[56]

Is this medievalism? The past of which Gildas writes does not really count as 'the Middle Ages'; nor does he write from any kind of post-medieval perspective. Nevertheless, his painful consciousness of the ways the country itself has both a national character that implies continuity with the past, as well as a history that is layered with different cultural and spiritual traditions, certainly anticipates one of the foundational practices of the medievalist imaginary: making the past still visible, tangible and memorable in the present, especially in the same *place*. This is comparable to the idea of pre-colonial, colonial and post-colonial practices being equally present in postcolonial societies. This is made more legible in Gildas's text through the device of *occupatio*: his refusal to condemn the errors of paganism and its visible traces in the landscape, and even more perversely, his refusal to *call out upon* the animist landscape, raising but resisting the possibility of dialogue with the spirits of mountains, fountains and hills. Gildas's emotional writing can be read as an early example of medievalism's interest in holding different temporalities and cultural patterns in complex and subtle suspension; and not just as an epistemological but also as an emotional and affective response. It is significant as an early and deeply self-conscious evocation of the layered cultural and temporal practices of sixth-century Britain. Sarah Semple tells a slightly different story about this kind of temporal and cultural layering in Anglo-Saxon history.[57] Drawing on evidence from burial practices, domestic and ecclesiastical settlements, place names and other written sources, she shows how Anglo-Saxon communities recycled prehistoric burial mounds and barrows, as well as Roman monumental remains, for example, in creative and 'theatrical' ways that indicate 'the intentional symbolic construction' of individual and community identity.[58] In contrast to these adaptive funerary practices, Gildas's writings are a model of cultural discontent.

As might be expected, medieval fictions, as opposed to histories, provide even more fertile ground for the kind of temporal and cultural shifting that characterises the medievalist imaginary. The much later romance of *Sir Orfeo* – a fourteenth-century rewriting of the Orpheus myth – exemplifies many of the practices we characterise as medievalist. It offers an early instance of portal medievalism, in Orfeo's entry to the magic land of faery (where the faery king's captives lie in a kind of temporal suspension, halfway between life and death); but at a more complex level, it is also structured around the possibility of layered or grafted cultures and the insouciant play with both its source material and the established conventions of time and space.

As other commentators have noted, the poem is itself a graft – like the grafted orchard tree under which Queen Eurodys falls asleep – of a rewritten rescue story with a happy ending, linked to a second classical-medieval narrative: the testing of the faithful steward.[59] In this version, Eurodys does not die of a snakebite, but is forewarned in a terrifying vision as she takes a midday sleep in the orchard that the king of faery will come and abduct her the next day. Despite being well-guarded, she is indeed abducted, and King Orfeo then leaves his kingdom in the hands of his steward, and exiles himself to the wilderness, where time and rough living take their toll on his body. After ten years, he comes across his wife riding with a faery company, and eventually he finds his way through a cleft in a rock into the land of faery. This kingdom is represented as a luminous medieval court, so bright, during both night and day, that it hurts the eyes. After being welcomed as a minstrel, and playing his harp, he persuades the Faery King to release his queen. Unlike classical versions of the myth, there is no prohibition about looking back, and Orfeo and Eurodys return home where the steward is tested and found faithful. We are told he will then inherit the kingdom after the childless couple die.

The intractability of this material has become something of a critical commonplace.[60] Jeff Rider suggests that the key transformative element here was its generic re-figuring in an intellectual and cultural climate whose dominant reading has been to allegorise: 'The most fundamental and important element in the remythification of the tale was the poet's decision to rewrite an allegorized (and increasingly Christianized) myth as a Breton lay.'[61] But Derek Pearsall argues that the Celtic Otherworld does not lend itself to Christian allegoresis in the same way that classical versions of the underworld might and that the very topic of the poem is 'unknowableness'.[62] Others, too, have remarked on the irreducible nature both of the faeries and the occulted world that they inhabit.[63]

We would argue that the poet's freedom with both story line and interpretative tradition vis-à-vis this 'other' space anticipates the imaginative freedom with sources and inherited tradition of much medievalist re-writing. We might even argue from the model of *Sir Orfeo* that to get things 'wrong', in temporal and cultural terms, and to change traditional narrative patterns, as modern popular medievalism often does, is to perform an aspect of medieval imaginative practice. The poet freely condenses classical genealogies and collapses both time and space as well as changing the ending as it appears in Ovid. After the poem's opening nod to the Breton lay's conventions of oral transmission, he introduces his main character:

> Orfeo was a king,
> In Inglond an heighe lording,
> A stalworth man and hardi bo;
> Large and curteys he was also.
> His fader was comen of King Pluto,
> And his moder of King Juno,
> That sum time were as godes yhold
> For aventours that thai dede and told.
> This king sojournd in Traciens,
> That was a cité of noble defens –
> For Winchester was cleped tho
> Traciens, withouten no.[64]

This passage richly encrusts several layers of cultural allusion. First, Orfeo is a king, whereas in prior versions he is primarily and emblematically a musician. The poet locates him securely in England – itself an act of cultural *translatio* – and describes him in vocabulary that brings together the honorifics of English heroic and French chivalric tradition. The first temporal loop is tossed up when Orfeo's ancestry is named as deriving from both Pluto and Juno. In Ovid's story, Pluto is the king whom Orpheus visits: if we were to layer these different accounts together, we could read a kind of Oedipal return to the father, who gives life both to the king and then the king's wife. In the English poem, moreover, the king's English royal line is traced back to Pluto and Juno in a move reminiscent of the *Gawain*-poet's derivation of Britain from Trojan Brutus. We are invited to put this story back into England's pagan past, perhaps a Christian re-writing of Roman polytheism. Lest we might doubt this genealogy, the poet reassures us *not* that the king of England had a classical past, but that English people in the past were in the practice of mythologising and deifying their heroes. We note the emphasis on story-telling among Orfeo's great ancestors, as part of the insistence on the transmission of narrative, and this poem's insistence on the good welcome a king should lay out for poets and musicians. It is a further tightening of the story's thematic and narrative loops that associate heroism with narrative *and* musical competence. Juno and Pluto are presented here as the author-heroes of Breton lays: 'for aventours that thai dede and told'.

The most egregious example of temporal, cultural and spatial pleating appears at lines 49–50, in which we are told simply that 'Winchester was cleped tho / Traciens, withouten no'.[65] This is the first time that Winchester is mentioned in the poem. Thrace is the city in which Ovid places Orfeo, but it is here mapped onto the prosperous and politically foundational English city. King Alfred was crowned in Winchester in 871 CE, and it was of course the site of Edward I's enormous Arthurian round table, at most only around fifty years old at the time of the poem's composition. With a simple speech act, mysteriously transmitted from the past – Winchester was *then* called Traciens – the poet confirms the English medievalising process in these lines, bringing together ancient Greece and medieval England in a doubled pleating of time and space. All it takes is a simple act of will and imagination that leaves no room for dispute: 'withouten no'. This defiance is analogous, we suggest, to the vision that produces Morris's neo-medievalist future, or the blow on the head that lands a Connecticut Yankee in the court of King Arthur: it is the work of authorial imagination that is presented for the reader's acquiescence. Similarly, when Orfeo sees Eurodys out riding with a group of ladies, he follows her through a simple portal, through a rock (probably a cave):

> In at a roche the levedis rideth,
> And he after, and nought abideth[66]

The poet is less interested in the portal than the world beyond, where it is always bright sunlight, where the castle walls shine like bright crystal, and the buttresses and pillars are adorned with gold. This medievalist portal into the faery kingdom is also easier to pass through than the fortified entrance of the medievalised castle: Orfeo must seek entrance from the porter, offering his services as a minstrel.

There is a further layer of mystification in the poet's earlier emphasis on the lay's Breton origins:

> In Breteyne this layes were wrought,
> First y-founde and forth y-brought,
> Of aventours that fel bi dayes,
> Wherof Bretouns maked her layes.
> When kinges might ovr y-here
> Of ani mervailes that ther were,
> Thai token an harp in gle and game
> And maked a lay and gaf it name.[67]

The source, then, for this anachronistic mapping of classical Greece onto medieval England is the conveniently vague Breton lay, with its tales of 'mervailes'.

Sir Orfeo thus puts in place a number of features we will come to associate with medievalism: an interest in the marvellous; a confident, if not wilful, eagerness to juxtapose different time zones and cultural spaces; an ease with representing and modifying past stories; and most importantly of all, an insistence that the past can be brought into the present, both temporally and spatially. In truth, the naming of the setting as Winchester is probably less important to the medievalising of the poem than its mise-en-scène: in spaces such as the orchard, the medieval city, the faery king's court and its hunting parties, and the testing of the steward motif that is familiar from romances such as *King Horn* and *Havelok the Dane*. But the very Englishness of the medievalisation here is an important component of the mechanics of temporal switching in *Sir Orfeo*.[68] The poem demonstrates a number of strategies for pleating time and space, and for moving in and out of medieval temporalities. We are not so much arguing for its influence on later medievalist texts as suggesting that the seeds of difference between the medieval and the non-medieval are already sown within medieval literature; and, most significantly, that the interpretative sets for reading both forms of temporal practice need not be radically different from each other.

Our second example of temporal switching is the fourteenth-century alliterative poem *St Erkenwald*. This work boldly brings different temporal moments together, but in a radically ahistorical manner, clustered around the site of a mysterious tomb. St Erkenwald became Bishop of London in 675 CE, though the poem introduces this time as 'noȝt full long sythen / Sythen Crist suffrid on crosse'; the repetition of 'sythen' helping to mask and displace the poet's 'foreshortened' chronology.[69] Erkenwald presided over the rededication of St Paul's cathedral. It had reverted to 'hethen' in the time of Hengist (fifth century), awaiting the arrival of St Augustine of Canterbury (in 597). The opening of the poem has condensed time, to situate St Erkenwald close to the time of the Crucifixion, but then expanded that time so that it may contain a long relapse into paganism and then two waves of reclaiming England for Christianity. Strictly, then, the medieval here does not know itself; does not know how old it is. As is the case in many a modern medievalist narrative, accurate temporal sequencing is less important than the evocation of narrative drama, in this case, Augustine's recasting of pagan temples:

[He] conuertyd all þe communnates to Cristendame newe.
He turnyd temples þat tyme þat temyd to þe deuell,
And clansyd hom in Cristes nome and kyrkes hom callid;
He hurlyd owt hor ydols and hade hym in sayntes
And chaungit cheuely hor nomes and chargit hom better:
Þat ere was of Appolyn is now of Saynt Petre,
Mahoun to Saynt Margrete oþir to Maudelayne,
Þe synagoge of þe Sonne was sett to oure Lady,
Jubiter and Jono to Jhesus oþir to James.
So he hom dedifiet and dyght alle to dere halowes
Þat ere wos sett of Sathanas in Saxones tyme.[70]

The poet then explains that London was at that time called 'the new Troy'.[71] At other points in the poem, however, the city is named simply as 'Troy':[72] a condensation of classical and medieval past that is comparable to the Winchester–Thrace renaming in *Sir Orfeo*. In this slippage, the distinction between the old and the revivified (or the classical and the medieval classicising) is carelessly blurred; another example of medieval ease with 'anachronistic' temporal layering.[73]

The text strikes a further note of temporal disunity in this possible allusion to the Appellants' charge against Nicholas Brembre, that as Mayor he planned to 'destroy the name of the Londoners' (nomen Londoniarum delevisse meditatus fuerat) by renaming the city 'Little Troy' (Parva Troia).[74] In fact, the name change was never formally promulgated but the threat of this change was obviously disturbing. It is a further indication of how mixed is the medieval use of the past: 'Troy' looks back nostalgically to the glamour of the classical past and calls up the honoured genealogy celebrated in *Sir Gawain and the Green Knight*; but at the same time, it recalls the 'trammes of treson' of that poem's opening lines and the destruction of a city state.

While we acknowledge the interpretative complexities raised by both these poems, the point we want to make here is a relatively simple one. These poems are interested in juxtapositions that foreground temporal, social and cultural changes or differences *within* medieval culture. The strict observation of historical and geographical accuracy or linear temporal sequencing is often of no greater interest to medieval writers than it is to the authors of modern medievalist fictions, who embrace fantasies of time travel or ignore the hard-won findings of historical scholarship and knowledge about the past. We suggest, however, that when medieval scholars deride medievalist fictions for this same kind of imaginative play with multiple or layered temporalities, they are condemning them for features that are utterly medieval.

Medievalism isn't always or only about the historically medieval; and the medieval and the medievalist are not always organised in a straightforward linear sequence, or a simple relationship of cause and effect. Rather, medievalism is a cultural, imaginative and, above all, transformative practice, one that is structured around a range of temporal, cultural, political and affective reflexes. Many of these reflexes are well-established patterns of cultural history that have produced a deceptively simple idea of modernity as having overcome its medieval past, and of medievalism as a simple nostalgic regression.

Conversely, these examples suggest that the relationship between the medieval and the medievalist has become part of a broader strategy of cultural othering – a use of the past to separate and distinguish even as such distinctions melt into one another. It is a temporal reflex that is entranced not just by the glamorous trappings of chivalry or the dark tourism of the premodern abject, but by the possibilities of traversing multiple and layered temporalities, and of imagining different forms of cultural otherness, of feeling our way into the past. As a form of cultural, imaginative and affective practice, its lineaments are familiar from medieval culture. And thus the medieval and medievalist imaginary, while not the same, overlap, both temporally and spatially.

More pragmatically, we suggest that to read both medieval *and* medievalist texts is to understand that if the spaces of the medieval and the medievalist overlap, then one does not traverse temporalities only by an act of interpretive will from a resolutely modern position. It is not just, as David Matthews demonstrates, that it is impossible to draw a firm dividing line between the work of editorial reconstruction and the creation of a post-medieval artefact (for example, the modern edition of a medieval text);[75] but rather, that the space of the past might at times turn up unbidden, breaking through into the present.[76] Further, that past may not be the past that we think about in conventional historical terms – the narration of things that have actually happened – but may well be the imagining or imaginings of alternative pasts projected into the future.[77]

Every work of literature, whether medieval or modern, imagines a range of futures for itself. This imagination is sometimes expressed directly, as in Chaucer's famous envoi, 'Go, litel bok', and his commissions to Gower and Strode at the end of *Troilus and Criseyde*, or Criseyde's prophetic exclamation about her own reputation into the future: 'O, rolled shal I ben on many a tonge!'[78] In terms of reader reception, too, Seth Lerer diagnoses the way Chaucer managed to infantilise his readers, with a profound effect on the first generations of response to his work.[79] There are also other less tangible possibilities. To put it in somewhat different terms, if we entertain the possibility that the material object known as the book is the 'death of the work rather than its inception', then these alternative possibilities appear like semiotic ghosts and revenants, existing in another realm.[80] The reception history of medieval literature suggests how emotional responses to medieval things are very difficult to disentangle from the medievalist emotions that drive the invention and recreation of the post-medieval. These phenomena all demonstrate the problem of defining what it is we are doing and how we are feeling when we work with medieval things: are our actions recuperative? Or creative? Or is this binary inimical to compassing the medieval?

Notes

1 Foucault, 'Questions on geography', p. 70.

2 For Michael Alexander, for example, the progression from ancient to medieval and modern has been 'axiomatic' (*Medievalism*, p. xxvii): in spite of modern recognition that such periodisation is a projection of historiography.
3 Jones, 'Early modern medievalism', p. 89.
4 For a recent understanding of medievalism as a primarily ideological practice, see Matthews, *Medievalism*.
5 For example, Simpson, *Reform and Cultural Revolution*; Strohm, *Theory and the Premodern Text*; Cohen, *Medieval Identity Machines*; Dinshaw, *Getting Medieval* and *How Soon Is Now?*; Holsinger, *The Premodern Condition*; Scala and Federico (eds), *The Post-Historical Middle Ages*; and Davis, 'The sense of an epoch'.
6 Many scholars have grappled with the niceties of terminology here. One of the most useful accounts is Utz, 'Coming to terms'.
7 Haydock, *Movie Medievalism*, p. 12.
8 Davis and Altschul, 'The idea of "the Middle Ages"', p. 1.
9 Trigg, 'Walking through cathedrals'.
10 The beginning of the so-called spatial turn probably began with Foucault and Henri Lefebvre, but its articulation is generally credited to Edward Soja in *Postmodern Geographies*.
11 Wells, *The Time Machine*, p. 6. See also the discussion of this passage in Haydock, *Movie Medievalism*, p. 75. Haydock makes the point that Wells 'describes time travel in cinematographic terms'.
12 For medieval studies see, for example, Matthews, *The Making of Middle English*; Utz, *Chaucer and the Discourse of German Philology*; Patterson, *Negotiating the Past*; Trigg, *Congenial Souls*; and several key essays in Ruggiers (ed.), *Editing Chaucer*. For medievalism studies see, for example, Chandler, *A Dream of Order*; Matthews, *Medievalism*; Wawn (ed.), *Northern Antiquity*; and D'Arcens, *Old Songs in the Timeless Land*.
13 See, for example, Brooks, *The Gothic Revival*.
14 See Matthews, *Medievalism*, pp. 125ff.
15 Morris's view of the Middle Ages has generally been seen as being at odds with Twain's pessimistic medievalism in *A Connecticut Yankee in King Arthur's Court*, but Morris and Twain admired each other. J. T. Boyd argues that Twain's work is sympathetic to Morris's social and political thought ('Labor and revolt', pp. 73–94).
16 Morris, *A Dream of John Ball*, pp. 1–3.
17 Morris, *A Dream of John Ball*, p. 13.
18 Morris was well aware of the contradiction between his socialist views and his capitalist endeavours (as were his detractors). See Vaninskaya, *William Morris*, pp. 45–6.
19 Morris, *A Dream of John Ball*, p. 110.
20 Morris, *A Dream of John Ball*, p. 115.
21 Morris, *News from Nowhere*, p. 2.

22 Morris, *News from Nowhere*, p. 45.
23 Morris, *News from Nowhere*, p. 60.
24 Morris, *News from Nowhere*, p. 305.
25 Ingham, 'Making all things new', p. 481.
26 The phrase is Stephen F. Eisenman's ('Communism in furs', p. 106); Morris, 'Paper read', p. 127. For Morris's conception of history as a spiral and his intellectual debt to a wide variety of sources, including Augustus Pugin, Thomas Carlyle, John Ruskin and especially Karl Marx, see Eisenman, 'Communism in furs', p. 106.
27 'Doctor Who in the Middle Ages'.
28 There are, of course, rules that govern these portals – rules that are rather spectacularly broken when a little girl named Lucy walks through the back of a wardrobe in wartime England and discovers a faun. Ultimately, the narrative resolves itself in a medievalist conclusion (all four children, at the end of *The Lion, the Witch and the Wardrobe*, are crowned kings and queens), but the portal doesn't so much lead to another time, or even to a 'secondary creation' (as Tolkien noted), as to a place where different mythological, legendary and folk figures from different times are deployed in the interests of a sustained allegory (Carpenter, *The Inklings*, p. 223).
29 For example, the magic rings in C. S. Lewis's *The Magician's Nephew*; or the magical oak doors that appear and disappear, but always lead to the past, in Susan Cooper's *The Dark is Rising*; or the enchanted ring that transports the heroine of Tamara Gill's *Defiant Surrender* back to twelfth-century Cumberland. For further discussion, see Trigg, 'Medievalism and theories of temporality', pp. 196–209.
30 Indeed, this is part of Ingham's point in her discussion of utopia and the 'new' – it is always a bricolage of the past.
31 Morris, *News from Nowhere*, p. 32.
32 Twain, *A Connecticut Yankee*, p. 25.
33 Haydock, *Movie Medievalism*, pp. 36–78; D'Arcens, *Comic Medievalism*, pp. 112–35; and Bildhauer, *Filming the Middle Ages*, pp. 25–51. See also D'Arcens's entry on 'Presentism' in Emery and Utz (eds), *Medievalism: Key Critical Terms*, pp. 181–8.
34 See Carolyn Dinshaw's exemplary, influential and far-reaching discussion of this passage in *How Soon Is Now?*, pp. 105–8.
35 See, for example, Burke, *The Renaissance Sense of the Past*, discussed in Trigg, 'Medievalism and theories of temporality', pp. 198–9.
36 The most often cited explanation of Serres's idea of temporal pleating is from his conversation with Bruno Latour: 'Classical time is related to geometry, having nothing to do with space, as Bergson pointed out all too briefly, but with metrics. On the contrary, take your inspiration from topology, and perhaps you will discover the rigidity of those proximities and distances you find arbitrary. And the sim*pli*city, in the literal sense of the word *pli*: it's simply the difference between topology

(the handkerchief is folded, crumpled, shredded) and geometry (the same fabric is ironed out flat)' (Serres with Latour, *Conversations*, p. 60). See also Trigg, 'Medievalism and theories of temporality', pp. 196–201.
37 Latour, *We Have Never Been Modern*.
38 See Fabian, *Time and the Other*.
39 Cohen, *Medieval Identity Machines*; Dinshaw, *How Soon Is Now?*; and Strohm, *Theory and the Premodern Text*. For more specifically medievalist studies, see also the essays by Kathleen Davis, 'Time behind the veil', and Patricia Clare Ingham, 'Marking time'. See also Nadia Altschul, 'Transfer'.
40 Dinshaw, *How Soon Is Now?*, p. 58.
41 Dinshaw, *How Soon Is Now?*, p. 59.
42 Dinshaw quotes from Caxton's English translation of the Latin original: Jacobus a Voragine, p. 438.
43 Dinshaw, *How Soon Is Now?*, p. 59.
44 Dinshaw, *How Soon Is Now?*, p. 59.
45 Dinshaw, *How Soon Is Now?*, p. 104.
46 Green (ed.), *The Trotula*, p. 107.
47 At least one iteration of the story makes the miracle of the sleepers more obvious proof for the resurrection of the body by actually altering the source and reporting the sleepers' death. Ælfric repeats Maximian's claim that 'Nu we arison of deaðe and we lybbað' (*Ælfric's Catholic Homilies*, p. 248). (Now we rise from the dead and we live.)
48 Massey, *For Space*, p. 15.
49 Dinshaw, *How Soon Is Now?*, p. 59.
50 See for example, Paul James's anatomy of different modalities of time in *Globalism, Nationalism, Tribalism*, pp. 164–70.
51 Trilling, *The Aesthetics of Nostalgia*, p. 130.
52 Hanning, *The Vision of History in Early Britain*, p. 45.
53 Gildas, *The Ruin of Britain*, p. 13.
54 See Trilling for a sharp distinction between salvation history and heroic history (*The Aesthetics of Nostalgia*, p. 128).
55 Gildas, *The Ruin of Britain*, p. 17.
56 Gildas, *The Ruin of Britain*, p. 17.
57 Semple, *Perceptions of the Prehistoric*, p. 11.
58 Semple, *Perceptions of the Prehistoric*, pp. 60–1.
59 See, for example, Riddy, who writes of the way the story is 'grafted' onto Celtic narrative stock ('The uses of the past in *Sir Orfeo*', p. 7).
60 See, for example, Lerer, 'Artifice and artistry in *Sir Orfeo*', p. 92.
61 Rider, 'Receiving Orpheus in the Middle Ages', p. 355.
62 Pearsall, 'Madness in *Sir Orfeo*', pp. 54–5.
63 Spearing, 'Interpreting a medieval romance', p. 78; and more recently, Cartlidge, 'Sir Orfeo in the Otherworld', p. 226.
64 *Sir Orfeo*, lines 39–50.

The space of time and the medievalist imaginary 49

65 We adapt Michel Serres's explicitly temporal idea of the *pli* to space *and* culture (see note 36 above). The poem is preserved in three manuscripts, but the reference to Winchester appears only in the Auchinleck version (National Library of Scotland, Advocates' MS 19.2.1).
66 *Sir Orfeo*, lines 347–8.
67 *Sir Orfeo*, lines 13–20.
68 Scholars such as Thorlac Turville-Petre have long made the case for English identity as being part of the subtext of the poem (*England the Nation*, p. 116). Such arguments, though, tend to treat the text as a fairly straightforward historical continuation of Anglo-Saxon-Norman rivalry rather than a site for multi-temporal identities. See, for instance, Battles, '*Sir Orfeo* and English identity', pp. 179–211.
69 Burrow and Turville-Petre, *A Book of Middle English*, p. 203.
70 *Saint Erkenwald*, lines 14–24.
71 *Saint Erkenwald*, line 25.
72 *Saint Erkenwald*, lines 251, 255.
73 A number of critics have commented on the meta-temporality of the text. See, for instance, Otter, '"New Werke"', pp. 387–414; and Smith, 'Crypt and decryption', pp. 59–85. Philip Schwyzer describes the miraculously preserved body as 'wreaking havoc with the temporal equivalent of depth perception' as 'the Londoners in the poem experience not simply the simultaneous failure of living and historical memory but also a collapse of the distinction between these two modes of memory' ('Exhumation and ethnic conflict', p. 7). As Karl Steel comments, 'Its time is piled up, mixed, all moments touching' ('Will wonders never cease').
74 Federico, *New Troy*, pp. 1–2.
75 Matthews, Medievalism, 168.
76 This is akin to what Aranye Fradenburg has characterised as 'breakaway moments' – 'the subject's intuition of being inhabited by a thing, something or someone unknown, a stranger, an uncanny neighbor (*Nebenmensch*). Is this Thing inside us, or are we inside it?' (Fradenburg, *Sacrifice Your Love*, p. 20). See also Ingham, *The Medieval New*, pp. 45, 138.
77 Compare Isidore's definition of history (by way of Cicero) as 'narratio rei gestae' (a narration of deeds accomplished).
78 Chaucer, *Troilus and Criseyde*, book V, lines 1786, 1856–7, 1061.
79 Lerer, *Chaucer and His Readers*, pp. 86–7.
80 Smith, 'The inhumane wonder of the book', p. 362.

2
Wonderful things

There are medieval things, like the old chair we discuss in the introduction, that seem to be conjured by texts, but in this chapter we would like to look at how medieval things – specifically, relics – can conjure, or, perhaps more accurately, bewitch texts. Whether these things were parts of a human body or objects associated with saints or items connected to Christ's time on earth, these relics of the past seemed to effect a kind of temporal miracle: making that past present. At the same time, the possibility of being deceived by a 'false' relic could confound the difference between old things and modern things in a confusing way: an anxiety we argue has been exemplary in the development of the relation between the medieval and the medievalist. We will suggest here that English reformers in the sixteenth century – a most formative time for medievalism as the study of a discontinuous past – took special interest in these relics because the supernatural presence they conjured was a challenge to their capacity to reconfigure or reform the past. Their main point of attack was to claim that these objects were exactly what they seemed – a bone, a lock of hair, a piece of wood – and that the representations made about them were false.

Such relics became synecdoches for the falsehoods of the past – things best forgotten or even destroyed because of the specious claims that humans had thrust upon them. The reformers' reading of the past here is monolithic. Attempting to discredit earlier relationships to certain kinds of objects by 'getting back' to what these objects actually were allowed reformers to claim that their project was epistemological, the triumph of truth over fabulous error. Yet what it actually accomplished was the destruction of the objects that led to this truth. In the spirit of the recent theoretical return to the ontology of the object, we suggest that getting back to the medieval object in this case might well be a way to get back to the history of medievalism. We further suggest that the binary of medievalism/medieval itself at once depends on and undermines a series of other binaries: truth/fiction, history/romance and signifier/signified. These binaries, as we will see, inform medieval, post-medieval and even late-modern epistemological approaches to history. This chapter thus turns to a close examination of some less familiar territory in the history of medievalism: the anxious narratives of reformation.

The 'lyveley memoryalles' of the past

While it would be too much to claim that the reformers consciously destroyed the past in order to recover it, the effect of this loss of the past was the same. Responding to Archbishop Parker's request in 1568 for information about the existence of 'ancient records and monuments', Bishop Robinson reported that many of the documents, records and monuments had vanished or, worse yet, been destroyed in the interests of the Reformation: 'There is not in this country any monuments of antiquity left, but certain fabulous histories and that lately written.'[1] In a historical irony, English antiquarians were alerted to the value of the medieval past at the same time as, and because it was being destroyed by, the dissolution of the monasteries and other Tudor 'reforms'.[2] James Simpson has argued that there were two related but distinct reactions to this loss: a melancholic reaction (embodied in John Leland) in which the civic humanist attempted to recuperate the lost history of Britain; and a reformist reaction in which men like John Bale attempted to 'delineate a Protestant literary tradition that extends back across the historical divide on which Bale thinks he is writing'.[3] As Aranye Fradenburg has suggested, reactions to loss inevitably involve the recreation of the lost object as 'a fantasy object, the product of the grieving subject's wishful fiction-making'.[4] If we think of this as a recreation of a past that existed before the destructive impulses of the Reformation, this sounds an awful lot like a form of medievalism. In this case, however, there seems to be some disagreement about what exactly has been lost. For Leland and perhaps a larger humanist tradition, the loss involves the records of historical succession – that which was actually reported as happening. For Bale and other reformers, it was somewhat different. Bale anxiously bewailed the loss of what he called 'the lyvely memoryalles of our nation', but he also says that he seeks to bring forth 'bookes out of the deadly darknesse to lyvele lyght'.[5]

As Bale's metaphor of light and darkness suggests, the creation of this divide in England was validated both by epistemological and religious rhetoric. One might use older sources (though not everyone was in agreement about their worth), but to engage in older practices was often regarded as a retreat into 'the distance and ... the dark' rather than seeing it from the 'position of light'.[6] This conceptual separation of an enlightened Renaissance from a dark Middle Ages is now seen as crucial both to the formation and abjection of the category known as the 'medieval'. Simpson gives voice to the continuing influence of this split when he observes that 'the "medieval period" continues to figure all that is other to modernity'.[7]

Of course, the persistence of the past proved troublesome, and the scope of the project of reform suggests just how uneasy the reformers were. Some wished simply to efface the medieval past, and hence advocated the destruction of all monuments that would lead to any memory of that time. Stephan Batman, domestic chaplain to Matthew Parker, the Archbishop of Canterbury and part of the circle surrounding Parker that was involved in salvaging the contents of monastic libraries, famously took issue with this wholesale condemnation:

> Bookes of Antiquiti are welbe stowed one those whose Sober staied mindes can abyde the redyng/but commonly Frantik braines suche az are more readye to be prattlers than / parformers / seing this book to be olde / Rather take it for papisticall / then else. & so many bookes com to confusion / S.B. Minister[8]

As Jennifer Summit has pointed out, the way that these Protestant preservers of old books dealt with the Catholicity of these sources turned on the ability to winnow truth from error and add copious annotation to these texts in order to ensure 'the complete elimination of the fabulous'.[9] In this, religious belief and humanistic method seem to converge in order to produce a re-formed memory of the past that was 'true and historical'. As suggested earlier, this lost past was itself a fantasy, but a fantasy that made its case for being true by debunking the demonstrably false. In other words, the great attraction of this lost object was based on the 'fact' that it was not a fantasy, but a real representation of the past because its very construction was built on the idea of rejecting falsehood. This truth depended on methods that seem closer to modern historical methods of recuperating a past than medievalism.

But what did this truth rely on? If it was epistemological in nature, it depended on the idea that there were certain things about the past that were demonstrably false (or in their terms 'fabulous') and so recovering those falsehoods was desirable insofar as those falsehoods could be debunked. Most treatments of what Bishop Robinson called 'fabulous histories' identify them as romances – those writings that were composed (as Roger Ascham said), for 'the moste parte in Abbayes, and Monasteries, a very likely and fit fruite of such an ydle and blynde kinde of lyvinge'.[10] These romances were seen as texts which busied the mind of their readers, distracting them from 'serious, and graver matters ... by delighting their fansies with such fabulous and ludicrous toys'.[11] But as Tiffany J. Werth has demonstrated, the seductive power of the fabulous not only distracted one from serious matters (such as religion), but it '"bewitched" readers in the same manner as did the "*Legendawry*" and "Saintes lyues"', hence explaining why romances were so often coded as 'papistical'.[12] Alexandra Walsham has shown how porous is the boundary between religious artefacts and 'material manifestations of the act of remembrance'.[13] At the same time, there was a fundamental difference between the 'dangerous' genre of romance and the genre of hagiography. The secular relics of romance (the Round Table at Winchester, Gawain's skull, Craddock's mantle, Lancelot's sword) activated a kind of belief that is memorial in structure. In other words, the physical object acted as a material *aide mémoire*. A religious relic, on the other hand, was something that was, as Walsham has demonstrated, ontologically different. It was 'an actual physical embodiment' of divine presence.[14] The belief was that power resided in the object itself.[15]

Religious relics 'presented a narrative of stasis in place of horrifying change: the end of this life and bodily decomposition'.[16] If mourning and melancholia are symptoms of trying to recreate the lost object, the medieval Church claimed that to possess a relic was not to lose the object at all. The remains of the body did not signify loss, but presence. As long as these relics existed, the Church claimed, we would have a supernatural communion with the succession of holy men and women who were venerated as saints. As long as these objects existed, the history of the Church did not need to be re-formed because it was continually present.

Of course, this is to fall into the trap of the reformers and code medieval belief as monolithic and absolute. In reality, the medievals actually maintained a healthy suspicion about the truth-claims of relics, a suspicion that is evident in the texts and stories that were produced to legitimate their provenance. Steven Justice has suggested that the attitudes towards the miracles associated with relics indicates a deep, if diffuse, scepticism both about relics and larger and more profound theological matters.¹⁷ The fact that these legitimating narratives were often themselves creative fictions further problematises our understanding of how medieval men and women interacted with these sacred objects. Indeed, one might well ask (in the face of this seemingly endless need for historical if medievalist bona fides), how did these objects retain their power? As Robyn Malo has argued, relic discourse is remarkable for its persistence during the period of reform. We argue that to understand this paradox we need to acknowledge that belief and disbelief are not binaries, but conditions or attitudes that one might well hold at the same time. We need to entertain the possibility that belief could be a kind of receptive performance in response to the religious theatre surrounding relics and that the very implausibility of relic discourse was simultaneously its greatest strength.

Medieval doubts about relics were clearly expressed in Guibert of Nogent's attack on their authenticity in the twelfth century when he noted that

> the clergy of Constantinople claim to possess the head of John the Baptist, yet the monks of Angers maintain the same claim. What greater absurdity, therefore, can we preach concerning this man, than that both these bodies of clergy should assert him to have been two-headed? ... But wherefore speak I of the Baptist's head, when I hear the same tale daily concerning innumerable saints' bodies?¹⁸

These doubts reached deep into medieval fictions: in both Giovanni Boccaccio's *Decameron*, which expressed grave misgivings about the provenance of relics; and Geoffrey Chaucer's *Pardoner's Tale*, in which the relic trade is characterised as nothing more than a bad confidence trick practised by corrupt ecclesiastical officials.¹⁹ For Malo, these examples are not only meant to satirise the transformation of relics into filthy lucre, but are part of a more general occlusion of the relics themselves as they are hidden away in more and more elaborate reliquaries. Her argument is meant to suggest that the personal relationship with the saints – the individual's feeling of the saint's presence or *praesentia* – may have been problematised by the increasing focus on that which contained the relic. We will have more to say about this later, but for now it is enough to suggest that the focus on the shrines and reliquaries might well be said to mitigate the possibility that they were fakes.

It was the genius of late reformers to exploit these doubts about the material remains of the medieval (and earlier) times, short-circuiting the temptation for the pilgrim to equate physical distance with historical distance. These reformers focused less on the ability of relics to connect men and women with the sacred past (though this was undoubtedly their goal) than on the *already accepted fact* that many of these remains were inauthentic. Crucially, however, they did not dismiss all relics as false. In 1536, for instance, the reforming bishop of Salisbury, Nicholas Shaxton, promised that after all relics in his jurisdiction were delivered to him, 'those [relics] that be esteemed and judged to be undoubtedly true relics, ye shall not fail at convenable time to have again'.[20] What reformers banked upon, then, was the idea that people would forget what they already knew (that many relics were false) so that false relics (like the infamous Rood of Boxley) could stand in synecdochal relationship to all relics. In a sense, the relic trade – the ultimate form of medievalism in that it helped modern things 'pass' as old – was now transformed into a weapon against the medieval. The reforming response to relics was, in turn, to make manifest their medievalness, in their abjectness, their falseness and their revelation of a backward-thinking mind.

The space of the recovery of this past could be quite sophisticated, yet despite the care with which some of these saints' lives and the *inventiones* (stories about the discovery of relics) that went along with them were cultivated, they were, for the most part, derided by early humanists. Erasmus claimed that they were 'old wives' tales' and even Thomas More declared early in his career that there was scarcely one saint's life that was not uncorrupted by some pious fraud.[21] Joseph Levine suggests why Erasmus and More might have rejected these fabulous histories. As he puts it, 'the new historiographical sciences that they [humanist historians] invented under the name of philology and antiquities were all predicated on the conviction that truth could be winnowed from error and that the effort was worth making'.[22] The appearance of historiographical 'science' fits neatly into a humanist narrative that codes early modern learning as monolithic, the first stirrings of a post-medieval epistemology that rejects fiction and fable in favour of truth and history. Levine's distinction is overdrawn, of course; more the product of a late modern desire to establish the verities of contemporary historicism than the realities of Reformation historiography. But even as Reformation humanists attempted to abject the Popish past, they also attempted to link the Protestant present with the 'origins' of Christianity.

This moment is crucial because it signalled both an important move in the religious history of England, and also an attempt to transform the way history was perceived. Reformers here cast the medieval as always medievalising – always a recreation, always a restoration and hence false. When, for instance, Cromwell's agents came to question the white liquid that was said to be the Virgin's milk at Walsingham, they pressed the former sexton about whether he had 'renewed the liquid when it seemed likely to dry up'.[23] The suspicion is that human agency lies behind that which 'remains', restoring or renewing that remainder. Relics in this way of thinking become a kind of manmade parody of the supernatural. The medieval is collapsed with medievalism and in this collapse comes the abjection of both.

The perils of invention

Yet, as we suggested at the outset, the distinction between reformist and Catholic approaches to these objects was profoundly unstable. Those responsible for the display of relics were not unaware of potential doubts, and provided legitimating texts that offered putative proof of their authenticity. Such texts narrated how relics of the sacred past were often found in hidden, antique places and thus gave a provenance to the sacred object. The most well-known 'finding' or *inventio* was the discovery of that ultimate relic of salvation history, the True Cross. There were many iterations of this story, but the larger outlines of the episode are fairly consistent. Helena, Emperor Constantine's mother, was led by divine guidance to a place that 'was virtually forgotten'. After excavating the site and clearing the 'profane and polluting objects' (a statue of Venus and perhaps other pagan items) that the Romans had placed there to mislead people, she found not one, but all three crosses from Golgotha. Initially unable to tell the difference, she was once more granted divine assistance to identify the true one and bring it home to her son.[24] Other stories about the discovery of saints' bodies such as the second *inventio* of St Quentin and the *inventio* of St Benedict replicate the basic features of the finding of the Cross, saying that the burial place of the saint was forgotten and only found by miraculous means. As these stories narrate the finding of corruptible bodies, they often add that the corpse exuded a wonderful odour, to suggest the incorruptible nature of the relic.

These stories provided a provenance to the abbeys and monasteries desiring to become custodians of the relics in question, but they also demonstrated how delicate the medieval connection with the past was felt to be. For various reasons (invasion, conquest, fear of persecution) holy relics were said to be either hidden or lost. Sometimes they were found by accident during excavations. But more often they were discovered by visions, or voices, or incarnations of those from the past. In psychological terms these stories certainly could demonstrate the extent to which the past could be excavated and discovered on its own. But they could also demonstrate how the detritus of the past (especially the pagan past) could mislead (though, as we saw above, the story of St Erkenwald provides a powerful counter-narrative).

In order to dispel doubts about the ability of ecclesiastical authorities to discover the 'truth' of the past, despite the extent to which intervening history had covered it up, these stories often actively staged doubt in a relic's authenticity so as to dismiss doubt more emphatically. The Abbey of San Clemente a Casauria, for instance, claimed that it possessed the body of St Clement and that the Abbey's founder Louis II had encased it in an alabaster sarcophagus. The body was apparently lost, and the monastic chronicle narrates a drama in which the Papal Envoy arrives in 1104 to express doubt about the Abbey's claim that it possessed the corpse, saying that 'nothing would induce him to believe this, until the abbot promised to show him this most sacred body'. In the end, so the chronicle tells us, the tomb is found with an inscribed name and a body. At this point the narrative turns from the external need for the authenticating ritual to the mindset of the abbot himself – he is relieved, 'for he was now certain of what previously the doubts of many had rendered even him a little bit dubious'.[25] In this drama the doubts of the actors are given free play even as these doubts are shown to be groundless. The point of the narrative is clearly to render the Abbey's claim indubitable. But if we examine the circumstances surrounding the story, the interplay of doubt and belief becomes more equivocal. For it's now known that, if the Abbey possessed a relic of St Clement before 1104, it was extremely small.[26] Thus even if the story about the Papal Envoy is true, it means that at some point someone either consciously inscribed a false name on the tomb, or was somehow convinced to believe, or convinced themselves to believe, that the Abbey possessed a first-class relic. Belief, in a sense, was performed until its truth became manifest in the 1104 *inventio* and the doubts that were given voice in the narrative are traces of the moment when belief became fact.[27] In this particular case one might well see how belief comes, not from bad faith, but through desire for a certain state of affairs. The performance of belief thus leads to the thing desired: the materialisation of the body. The binary of truth and fiction is under pressure here, but less from what the reformers would characterise as wilful deceit and more out of good intention.

But what of instances in which the history of the relic is consciously confected? An explicit example of this tendency is the *passio* of Saints Alban and Amphibalus by a monk who refers to himself simply as William.[28] William tells us that he has discovered an '*anglico sermone*' by an unknown author that presents the story of St Alban (and his mentor, Amphibalus) apparently written in conjunction with the discovery of St Alban's body.[29] But the narrator of William's 'source' makes no claim to be an eyewitness to the persecution of the saint. Instead he recovers the story only because the citizens of the city in which the saint had been tortured (Verulamium) had written about the saint's passion on the city walls. Because the walls were crumbling and the story was about to be lost, William's source tells us that 'he has diligently researched and learned the entire sequence of events and, so that it might not be hidden from posterity [*ne lateret posteris*], I have taken pains to entrust it in this manner to pen and paper'.[30] In this narrative, the story of St Albans quite literally becomes the boundary that defines the city. Yet as the city itself falls into ruin, the spatialisation of time is betrayed by the medium that makes place possible. The text must be produced to preserve the text in the ruins, and then William must copy the text based on the text of the ruins (and the few oral witnesses) in order to preserve the story of the preservation of the story.

As Monika Otter has suggested, the recourse to an old manuscript and the emphasis on the thin genealogy of textuality might seem to suggest that 'William is consciously attempting to create historical depth by staggering time levels, creating, as it were, a three-dimensional rather than a flat picture of the past'.[31] Even the monks understood the fictive nature of the text. As Otter herself points out, two generations later Matthew of Paris invents a story (which is clearly based on the earlier story) about the finding of an old *vita* of St Alban (perhaps William's) that, after being translated by an old monk by the name of Unwona, falls to pieces. Contemporary readers might find these stories 'risible' and read them as self-referential narratives about the fragility of the past, but they operate with the doubleness we have already observed as both possible fictions and authenticating narratives.[32]

Like the complex temporal narratives we discussed in chapter 1, their value lies in their ability to be *like* the past even if they are not what one would consider accurate representations of the past. The past may be lost, but it may yet be recuperated even by means that are imaginative. It is difficult to know how those who confected these fictions felt about their recreations of the past. They might well have understood them as 'pious frauds', lies told in order to advance a greater cause. But we would like to entertain the possibility that, on some level, some believed their own stories because they related things that may very well have happened, or to put it in theological terms, even something that was more or less probable (even if not quite in the way they imagined it).[33] To believe in this probability would not put one in error and so one could well claim a kind of truth.[34]

The possibilities of analogical historical truth are most powerfully advanced in what we characterise as the verisimilar visions of the mystics, but even here we claim that the visions or confected stories that accompanied relics could merely be probable and lay claim to truth. Part of this power derived from the visions that often accompanied the 'finding' of relics.[35] But what set these objects apart from more mundane objects or images was their anterior history – the mystery of their origin and displacement. One could even argue that the supplementary power of the object derived from its hidden history: hence the need for these authentic fictions. The goal of these fictions, it should be noted, was to provoke wonder in their readers.[36] While this wonder was not necessarily at odds with what might be termed an epistemological response, its very nature was to challenge the boundaries of knowing so that belief was required.[37]

Such stories, surrounding and contextualising the object, might seem to act as placeholders, keeping objects from meaning things that we don't want them to mean. The physical manifestation of this narrative context for the relic was the reliquary and, for the more mundane historical object, the *Kunstkabinett* or later the museum. We might modify Eileen Joy's dictum about the function of the museum and say that the museum and the reliquary *attempt* 'to hold things in and keep them in their places'.[38] But the wonder that attends these objects made it possible for objects often to break free from their settings, or implicate the settings in their own mysterious history. So how does one get back to this 'mysterious' history? How can the reader recover the lost history of the thing that is by its very nature anterior?

Juliet Fleming has suggested that in order to recover the prehistory of the object we must 'avoid talking about representation and its surrogates' because to do so 'would short-circuit the whole enterprise'.[39] Presumably, she argues this because in a post-structural sense the situation of an object always already gestures to the ways in which it is non-situated. For instance, the framed setting of the reliquary situates the object, telling us what it is and what it is not. Yet as Seeta Chaganti has argued, such 'framing' inevitably draws attention to ways in which what is inside the frame cannot be sealed off from that which is outside it.[40] Quoting Derrida, she avers that 'the limit of the frame or border of the context ... always entails a clause of non-closure. The outside penetrates and thus determines the inside'.[41] The object in and of itself exists for us only insofar as the frame exists and yet this frame can never hold, situate or even 'mean' the object. For Fleming, the only way out of this inability to get back to the object is to put the question of representation under erasure.

Fleming's radical erasure of representation seems to go too far. It is tempting to take satisfaction in 'knowing the worst, which is that we cannot finally, Know',[42] but we advocate turning instead to what Paul Strohm characterises as the 'real promise of reclaiming ... provisional knowledge in the face of impossibility'.[43] Given that representation is all we really have, we suggest that the 'promise' might be found in wonder, in the dialectic between scepticism about and belief in representation. Our understanding of wonder is, then, at odds with those who have argued that the function of wonder in the Middle Ages was its own self-destruction and replacement by *scientia* or knowledge.[44] At the same time, we reject a radical scepticism that claims a fundamental inability to know. The truth, if we can use that term, lies in the neither/nor of wonder. It suspends the individual between knowing and not knowing precisely because the relationship to the object is a question of belief.[45] This belief, as we have also seen, was enabled by *inventiones*, stories that were confected in order to give credence to the belief that the thing was full of wonder. These stories at once represent objects and signal the extent to which objects exceed representation. This final slippage between the binary of signified and signifier might signal the extent to which any recuperation of the object ultimately inhabits the space of fictionality and falsehood; however, these *inventiones* also testify to the way subjectivities can enable unexpected connections to the past.

Contemporary invention, pleasure and the containment of the law

We turn once more to the language of affect here, suggesting that mood (what Heidegger calls *Stimmung* or collective attunement) might help us get at the subjectivity underlying belief in a truth that is not true. Moods, as Jonathan Flatley points out, 'are a kind of atmosphere, a kind of weather, they are not "psychological", located in some interior space we can reach by way of introspection or self-examination. Moods are not in us; we are in them; they go through us.'[46] They make us appreciate 'the extent to which we have been thrown into a world that is the way that it is and not some other way'.[47] As we have seen, post-Reformation scepticism was enabled by its own mood – a deep and abiding suspicion of that which seemed 'fabulous'. The mood was pervasive enough to persist over a long period of time primarily because it fitted so well with notions of epistemological progress.

Even as affect studies have come into vogue, the current mood of literary and historical studies could still best be called 'critical'. Medieval studies is no different – fabulous narratives, like the subjects of psychoanalysis, are treated as 'symptomatic fictions laid out for diagnosis'.[48] Questions of belief or affect are broken down to reveal hidden aetiologies. As Rita Felski has pointed out, the suspicious stance of this kind of critique often positions itself as 'moodless – dispassionate and thus epistemologically privileged'.[49] Such approaches are seductive in that they seem to avoid the confusing atmosphere of affect and afford a compelling clarity of the past. Yet critical detachment is not an absence of mood but simply another kind of mood that attempts the 'scission of thought from affect'.[50] Wonder at the past, on the other hand, is a mood that avoids an overly schematic distinction between mind and body, bringing thought and affect, knowing and feeling, together.[51] The promise of wonder is thus not epistemological certainty, but affective possibility.

This is not to say that there haven't been times when the mood seemed to change. The antiquarians' enthusiasm for the past (as we will see in chapter 4) was enabled by a mood that countered the prevailing mood of hermeneutical suspicion. And in imaginative terms there has been constant pressure on modernity's suspicious mood. The novels of H. Rider Haggard and Arthur Conan Doyle often rely on a romance structure that echoes the loss and finding of an object that we saw in the medieval sources. Most notably, at the end of the twentieth century this narrative structure was memorably transformed into a film that focuses on a pre-Christian relic – the Ark of the Covenant.[52] This film would initiate one of the most powerful cultural fantasies about our relationship to the artefactual past: the Indiana Jones franchise. This franchise focused on individual objects, the Ark, mystical Indian gems, the Grail, a crystal skull. But even a passing acquaintance with the movies reveals that their point of interest is the professor-hero, Dr Jones. The cinematic emphasis thus shifts from the found object to the finding itself. Human subjectivity and acquisition of knowledge lie at the heart of all of these films, whose subjective experience of objects does not merely mediate their power, but fulfils an anthropocentric fantasy about the construction of the world. Such cultural fantasies hardly seem the place to uncover an anterior history of objects. But these films also represent the extent to which objects *even in their representation* resist human efforts to frame them.

The first film establishes the basic pattern of the series and explicates the rationale of the historical relic. In a scene where Jones confronts his 'dark other', his rival, René Belloq, holds up a silver watch and compares it to what would be considered one of the greatest of relics: 'It's worthless. Ten dollars from a vendor in the street. But I take it, I bury it in the sand for a thousand years, it becomes priceless! Like the Ark. Men will kill for it; men like you and me.'[53] The initial part of the claim seems completely self-evident – but the second part seems ludicrous. The draw of the film is clearly tied to the importance of the Ark (*Raiders of the Silver Watch?*). So why have Belloq analogise the Ark and the watch? Psychoanalytically, of course, the object has power not because of what it is but what it represents. Žižek characterised this kind of object (what Alfred Hitchcock called the MacGuffin) as 'clearly the objet petit a, a lack, the left-over of the real, setting in motion the symbolic order, a pure semblance of the "mystery" to be explained, interpreted'.[54] The analogy of the watch and the Ark, then, depends not on their equivalence as objects, but on their equivalence as lack – that which cannot be represented, that which cannot be demystified or recovered.

As far as this goes, it makes good sense. If the object exists only as a kind of carapace and has meaning only insofar as we have the desire to penetrate beneath its surface, then it matters not whether the object is a watch or an Ark. The similar function erases difference. We might believe that the Ark is a fundamentally different class of object than the watch, but one forgets, because the film is so ingrained in popular culture, that there is an entire scene in which Jones and his colleague have to explain the 'history' of the Ark and its loss to two apparently religiously ignorant US agents. Like any other MacGuffin, the Ark needs human narration in order to become an object of desire. It certainly commands respect because of its connection to the Divine (something the movie insists on), but it is the romance of the 'loss' and 'finding' of the Ark that compels the viewer. This twentieth-century *inventio*, then, demonstrates the power of the object as it continually gestures to the failure of human attempts to circumscribe, use or even understand it (a theme that would be repeated in the third instalment of the series with that ultimate of relics, the Grail).[55]

On a more historically specific level, however, differences can matter a great deal. If one wishes to recover something more than the fundamentally irrecoverable nature of the Real, then one needs to be attentive to differences however small, or in this case, large. Belloq's analogy linking the watch and the Ark is actually a kind of thought experiment. Why are we drawn to the Ark? Were we to take an ordinary object, could we be equally drawn to it? His solution, to lose it and find it in a thousand years, suggests the extent to which time transforms an object (something emphasised by his choice of a time-keeping instrument) and to which the phenomenon of the *inventio* grants power. So far, the similitude of the objects seems assured, but one has to acknowledge that the Ark is different from the watch insofar as the Ark is not only a historical object (manufactured, assuredly, but more on that in a moment) but an object that contains another object – the two tablets of the Law. The watch is, or could be, enshrined in a narrative, but that narrative is not a thing in itself. By contrast, the Ark is *the* thing that everyone searches for in the movie despite the fact that it is a manufactured object (though the instructions for it come from God) and that what it holds is what is really important.

One could read this as an argument for belief in God. The film would thus enact a familiar medieval lesson: those who misuse sacred objects will answer to divine justice. But the movie is curiously resistant to such a moralistic conclusion. Instead we get the hero, quite frankly, in a mood. He acknowledges the power of the Ark but seems religiously *un*moved. His final comment is less about the power of God and more about the inability of humanity to compass the object ('Bureaucratic fools. They don't know what they've got there').⁵⁶ The film meditates on how the subjective inability to understand gives objects power. The only thing humans can do is categorise, place the object within a framework that does not explain but catalogues. Bureaucracy gets a bad name here, but the hiddenness of bureaucracy tames the power of the Ark by 'losing' it – the final joke being the wording on the outside of the crate (being buried in a warehouse of similar crates) saying 'Do Not Open'. The stones within the Ark have transformed the Ark into the thing itself. The only way to tame this power is to create another container and bury it amid a series of containers that are seemingly identical in a much larger container – to render the Ark indistinguishable from all other things and thus to maintain the equivalency of all things.

As we have seen, however, the priority of the thing being contained will always trump any attempt to contain the thing because the container is itself historically situated. That which is contained ultimately permeates and affects the container. The series of Chinese boxes thus becomes a kind of historical analogy that is materialised in the containers themselves. This is particularly evident in the medieval conception of the reliquary, which very early on was perceived as an analogy of the Ark of the Covenant.⁵⁷ The material tradition here gets analogised in the way we might think about history. In fact, the Ark was seen in early medieval exegesis as a figure for the unity of the two Testaments – the incorruptible wood of the Ark as an analogy to the incarnational flesh of Christ.⁵⁸

The past can never be completely contained. In the Middle Ages, the wood of the Ark represented the new promise of Christ's flesh but was also the container holding the older law which continually affected the disposition of the New. In a sense one could say that all history, not merely the history of the object, is necessarily contained in these Chinese boxes. Each manifestation of history, each slice, each frame alters the way we see the older bit, but the older bit in turn affects the disposition of the present that attempts to contain it. Through this constant interpenetration of the past and the present, each problematic attempt to compass the past would seem to open up the past to us, but also suggests that our relationship to the past is in some sense an infinite regression. Is there any way out of this insistent series of Chinese boxes?

It seems difficult. After all, if we return to the Ark, even the thing contained in the Ark is a manifestation of the object's entry into human history. And it is what it is because it is a medium for representation. In fact, the story about the Commandments is really about the entry of written law into society – the stones here are chosen presumably because of their durability. And their destruction and reinscription seem to demonstrate precisely the extent to which materiality is less important than the human abstraction that lends meaning to the tablets – something that becomes clear in the destruction of the golden calf, a material object of worship (but an idolistic representation). What seems important is the writing on the tablets. Power certainly devolves from the tablets insofar as God has touched them, but also in the extent to which they bear the timeless idea of the law. Inherent within this idea, of course, is denial – the 'thou shalt nots' that, as Fradenburg has suggested, sharpen our appetites and give us a form of pleasure. We enjoy, therefore, the abstraction of denial insofar as it structures desire. The story of the loss and finding of the object enacts our fantasy of the loss and finding of the historical past. But is this all it does? We must also acknowledge the enjoyment conveyed by the ways in which the material manifestations of the law (the tablets, the Ark) appear to be unregulated and inadequately captured by representation. The pleasure conveyed by the material medium here becomes a way for us to enter history not merely in figural or allegorical terms, but causally, in so far as the object exceeds narratorial attempts to comprehend it. The film, which narrates the loss, finding and loss of the Ark, places pressure on the suspicious mood of its hero and thus interrogates a wholly rationalistic and sceptical relationship to the world.

So can there be any true history of the object? Alexandra Walsham remarks:

> material remains have no intrinsic status as relics. The former become the latter as a consequence of the beliefs and practices that accumulate around them. They are the products and confections of the cultures that engender and reverence them. The making of them is both a social and a cognitive process. Outside the cultural matrix and environment within which they were created, they are inert and lifeless objects devoid of significance and worth.[59]

One could certainly see why Walsham and others would wish to make the claim that human agency determines the worth, value and agency of the object. The task of the historian then becomes clear. Like that of the reformer, it is to demystify the seemingly inexplicable power of the object by revealing the various forms of human agency underlying the object's manifestations.

It is certainly crucial to understand the various forms of agency that underlie the valuation of objects in the world. But, as we suggested above, to focus solely on the way hidden human agencies everywhere structure our relationship to the world is simply to substitute one belief system for another. As Jane Bennett puts it, 'this hermeneutics of suspicion calls for theorists to be on high alert for signs of the secret truth (a human will to power) below the false appearance of nonhuman agency'.[60] But, as has more recently become apparent, to treat everything everywhere as always concealing or somehow mimicking human agency is a reductive enterprise that reinforces a false dichotomy of surface/depth and does a very bad job of describing the world.[61] In this formulation, belief in the magic of objects becomes the product of mystification rather than a phenomenon in and of itself.

We would suggest a more sceptical treatment of scepticism and hence a more flexible understanding of objects. We cannot exactly recover the wonder of the medievals. But just as they believed in the efficacy of divine providence working through objects (even as they understood that not all of these objects were what they seemed to be), so we would argue that one can retain scepticism about the nature of these objects without dismissing (and hence abjecting) the basis for belief underlying these objects. Approaching objects, particularly sacred objects, that seem to provide a channel for power or be powerful in and of themselves without the fear of identifying with those we study might allow us to appreciate how objects orient subjects' relationships to the world in occult ways. We should, we think, be in the mood to encounter these objects. If we are less eager to demystify every relationship between subject and object, we will be more sensitive to ways in which certain beliefs might be merited, or at the very least, it may allow us to encounter the mystery of belief's residue. This affective state might be called the mood of medievalism, an analogy of how the medievals themselves felt when they approached sacred objects. It is post-medieval but has the virtue of offering a connection to the past rather than a desire to reform it.

Notes

1 Greg, 'Books and bookmen', p. 267. For a brief discussion of Robinson's comment and its relationship to 'monumentality' in the period, see Summit, 'Monuments and ruins', pp. 9–10.
2 Aston, 'English ruins and English history', pp. 231–55.

Wonderful things 67

3 Simpson, *Reform and Cultural Revolution*, p. 22.
4 Fradenburg, '"Voice Memorial"', p. 174.
5 Bale, quoted in Simpson, *Reform and Cultural Revolution*, p. 17.
6 Simpson, *Reform and Cultural Revolution*, pp. 27, 32.
7 Simpson, *Reform and Cultural Revolution*, p. 32. Biddick makes the point somewhat earlier in The Shock of Medievalism, p. 2.
8 Quoted in Langland, *Piers Plowman*, pp. 7–8.
9 Summit, *Memory's Library*, p. 121.
10 Ascham, *Toxophilus*, p. 17.
11 Harvey, *A Discursive Probleme*, K2v–3r.
12 Werth, *The Fabulous Dark Cloister*, p. 39. She is quoting Edward Dering here.
13 Walsham, 'Introduction', p. 13.
14 Walsham, 'Introduction', p. 12.
15 Cyril of Jerusalem was among the first to make this claim. See *A Select Library*, vol. 7, p. 138. Under pressure from the reformers, the Church would 'clarify' its position and move against the 'superstition' that the body itself contained power. At the final session of the Council of Trent (4 December 1568) the Church adopted a position close to Thomas Aquinas's – that God chose to work miracles in the presence of relics, but the object itself was mere matter (though worthy of honour).
16 Malo, *Relics and Writing*.
17 Justice, 'Did the Middle Ages believe in their miracles?', p. 21.
18 Guibert, *Treatise on Relics*, bk. 1, chap. i, col. 614.
19 Boccaccio expressed a hearty distrust of relics in the tenth tale of the sixth day of the *Decameron*, in the story of Ser Cepperello, where he claims that if we have erred in our veneration of a body as the body of a saint, 'we may recognize how very great is God's loving-kindness towards us, in that it takes account, not of our error, but of the purity of our faith, and grants our prayers even when we appoint as our emissary one who is His enemy' (*The Decameron*, p. 37).
20 Quoted in Marshall, 'Forgery and miracles', p. 58. The pilgrims who made their way to shrines at Walsingham and Canterbury understood all too well (as Peter Marshall puts it) that 'ostensibly sacred things *might* be fakes' ('Forgery and miracles', p. 41, our emphasis).
21 Marshall, 'Forgery and miracles', p. 45. See also King, *The Faerie Queene*, p. 180; Ferguson, *Utter Antiquity*, p. 124.
22 Levine, *Humanism and History*, p. 49.
23 Marshall, 'Forgery and miracles', p. 52.
24 'Constantine the Great', p. 85. Whatley's edition here is of Rufinus of Aquileia's version of the legend, which is the one that Aelfric chooses to translate.
25 For a treatment of these episode and this quotations, see Loud, 'Monastic chronicles', p. 110. The Abbey's claim was almost certainly false.

26 Loud demonstrates that, at best, the Abbey possessed a small relic of St Clement only after the 1104 *inventio*.
27 In a more modern context this disbelief mitigation works in contemporary films that 'need' to convince the viewer of the possibility of the supernatural. They often stage doubt through a sceptical character who is gradually convinced that events within the film elude a natural explanation. See Smuts, 'Haunting the house', pp. 158–73.
28 We depend on Monika Otter's fine work on *inventiones* here, particularly, '"New Werke"', pp. 387–415. Otter specifically mentions Geoffrey of Monmouth's invocation of an older source as the source for one of these narratives, the *passio* of Saints Alban and Amphibalus ('"New Werke"', p. 398).
29 Otter, '"New Werke"', p. 398.
30 Otter, '"New Werke"', p. 399.
31 Otter, '"New Werke"', p. 400.
32 Otter characterises one such fiction as 'risible' ('"New Werke"', p. 404).
33 The doctrine of probabilism, in which one could hold a position that was probable and not be in error, would not come into full force until the Renaissance. But in the fifteenth century, Jean Gerson explicitly suggests that those who believe in the authenticity of a certain relic, or disbelieve in that relic based on a *greater or lesser* probability that the relic was genuine, could not be held to be in error. See Elliot, 'Seeing double', p. 46, n. 88.
34 There were those, of course, who understood all too well that their pious frauds were simply false, though perhaps justified by the increase in devotion among, or alms from, the faithful.
35 Though these visions were often accompanied by a need for physical signs as well. One thinks of Einhard's *The Translations and Miracles of ... Marcellinus and Peter*, pp. 69–91.
36 See Koopman, *Wonderful to Relate*.
37 The most commonly used word was *admiratio* but the range and idea of wonder depended on the thing being wondered at (and the aims of the author). Wonder at natural marvels or magic could be considered different than wondering at miracles. For a treatment of the vocabulary of wonder as well as a discussion of the different deployments of wonder in miracle narratives see Rüth, 'Representing wonder', pp. 89–114. The compass of wonder – from that which enables belief to that which leads one to question the wonder itself – is evident in the injunction to tell only of wonders that are 'probable truths'. See Brewer, *Wonder and Skepticism*, pp. 110–11. The danger was excessive curiosity, which could lead not only to doubt, but disbelief in the idea of the miracle itself (Brewer, *Wonder and Skepticism*, p. 122; Justice, 'Did the Middle Ages believe in their miracles?', p. 18).
38 Joy, 'What counts is not to say', p. 29. See also Fleming's citation of Joy's claim and her critique of Cohen's appropriation ('Scraping by', p. 130).

39 Fleming, 'Scraping by', p. 128.
40 Chaganti, *The Medieval Poetics of the Reliquary*, p. 13.
41 Chaganti, *The Medieval Poetics of the Reliquary*, p. 13.
42 Strohm, *Theory and the Premodern Text*, p. 110.
43 Strohm, *Theory and the Premodern Text*, p. 110.
44 In her presidential address to the American Historical Association, Carolyn Walker Bynum asserted that 'wonder should lead to its own replacement by knowledge' ('Wonder', p. 4). For a critique of this view see Prendergast, 'Canon formation', p. 246.
45 For a somewhat different and perhaps more capacious understanding of this 'suspension', see Uebel, 'The pathogenesis of medieval history', p. 49.
46 Flatley, *Affective Mapping*, p. 22.
47 Flatley, *Affective Mapping*, p. 24.
48 Justice, 'Did the Middle Ages believe in their miracles?', p. 2.
49 Felski, *The Limits of Critique*, p. 25.
50 Felski, *The Limits of Critique*, p. 25.
51 Felski and Fraiman, 'Introduction', p. viii.
52 Susan Aronstein argues that this and the two films that follow it are parts of a chivalric trilogy that recall Arthurian narrative patterns (the Hero's Adventures in the Otherworld, the Quest for the Sacred Object, the Imprisoned Maiden). While we might not make claims about specifically Arthurian forms in these films, it's no accident that the telos of the trilogy leads its audience to knights, the salvific cup of Christ and the medieval (*Hollywood Knights*, pp. 122–33).
53 Spielberg (dir.), *Raiders of the Lost Ark*.
54 Žižek, 'Alfred Hitchcock', p. 8.
55 The Ark continually eludes attempts to categorise or use it. It burns off the swastika placed on the crate containing it. Despite Belloq's 'Jewish ritual' (an Aramaic passage that is sometimes spoken when the Ark that holds the Sefer Torahs is opened), he and the Nazis are destroyed, and the hero and heroine are saved only by voluntarily averting their eyes, thus acknowledging their inability to comprehend the Ark (Spielberg [dir.], *Raiders of the Lost Ark*).
56 Spielberg (dir.), *Raiders of the Lost Ark*.
57 Thunø, *Image and Relic*, p. 164.
58 Thunø, *Image and Relic*, p. 164.
59 Walsham, 'Introduction', p. 14. Walsham quotes Geary ostensibly to the same effect, but he is a bit more circumspect, claiming 'the bare relic – a bone or a bit of dust – carries no fixed code or sign of its meaning: divorced from a specific milieu it is unintelligible and incomprehensible' (*Furta Sacra*, p. 5).
60 Bennett, *Vibrant Matter*, p. xiv.
61 For an early treatment of the complexities and confusions of surface/depth see Strohm, *Theory and the Premodern Text*, p. 178.

3
Fear, error and death: The abjection of the Middle Ages

For all the sophistication of our theorising about the past, behind our stories of embarrassment, memory, loss, love and retrieval, there remains something intimidating and forbidding about the Middle Ages. Sealed off from modernity in its great oak chest of mythologised otherness, the medieval period still promises both a thrilling, gothic adventure and an epistemological challenge. Although scholars rarely acknowledge it, there are many aspects of medieval studies that have the capacity to strike fear and anxiety into the heart of anyone tackling the interpretation of medieval literature and culture, from aspiring student to learned professor. As a result of its deep imbrication with the technical disciplines of philology and palaeography, and in the shadow of its Latinate alterity from vernacular modernity, the study of the Middle Ages carries with it an almost overwhelming burden of authority and specialist expertise which has the potential to generate tremendous anxiety. All academic disciplines are competitive; but in the shrinking job markets of the humanities, the fear of being called out, of being exposed in error, is a growing threat. Medieval studies has specialised, moreover, in making students and scholars feel inadequate to the tasks they set themselves. Lee Patterson wrote in the 1990s about the imposing disciplinary requirements of medieval studies, implying that it is almost impossible to acquire all the languages, and all the skills in diplomatics and palaeography, and all the historical and cultural context that would seem to be required, according to the traditional hierarchies and expectations of medieval scholarship, before the act of critical interpretation can begin. (We might now add to this, a mastery of all forms of contemporary critical theory, the techniques associated with digital humanities and the capacity to use social media and other forms of outreach to convince universities and funding bodies of the urgency and significance of our work.)[1] Patterson argued that this insistence on specialist techniques is to some degree self-imposed: a result of the mixed blessing of the Renaissance construction of the medieval as marked by alterity, a field of cultural difference that requires reassembly. This alterity conferred an attractive and marked professional identity on medievalists, but resulted in a degree of defensiveness, as they surrounded themselves with this 'armature of scholarly techniques and abilities', and embraced a professional hierarchy that Patterson likens to a patriarchal apprenticeship system. As a result, 'medieval studies has traditionally policed itself with the spectre Error, every medievalist's nightmare: better to be dull than "unsound"'.[2]

We open this chapter by proposing that this expression of disciplinary power is an attempt to wall the scholarly study of the medieval off from the thrilling, dark, tortuous atavism of popular medievalism. In contrast to the well-established decorums and rules of academic scholarship, medievalism can range wildly in attitudes to historical truth, from the scrupulous research of re-enactors into medieval costume, images from medievalist film and fiction, to the lazy and inflammatory characterisations of contemporary Islam as being somehow 'medieval'. These slippages appear to threaten the cultural authority of the academy, but its attempts to police its borders have by and large been doomed to failure. We suggest that there is a structural dialectic in conceptions about the medieval past and its relation to the present: a dialectic that has the effect of drawing us in, affectively and emotionally, to the past, even if through the thrill of abjection, while at the same time pushing us away from any easy identification with its arcane difficulties.

Fear, error and fraud

What are the origins of this terror and anxiety about error: the fear of misreading or mismaking the medieval? Seth Lerer identifies the fear of scholarly and textual error as a Renaissance obsession, where it is closely bound up with the possibility of doctrinal error in an era where mistakes could be deadly.[3] It is an obsession given particularly grisly and gothic form in Spenser's medievalist *The Faerie Queene*, where Error is the first creature Red Cross Knight must conquer. Half woman, half serpent, Error is 'most lothsom, filtie, foule, and full of vile disdaine' (i.1.14).[4] She lurks in a cave in darkness, fearing the light, and feeding her thousand babies on her 'poisonous dugs'. As Red Cross enters the 'darksome hole', his armour sheds a little light on the dismal scene, but on seeing this gleam, Error's spawn creep back into her mouth. When he grips her throat, she vomits vilely:

> Her vomit full of bookes and papers was,
> With loathly frogs and toades, which eyes did lacke,
> And creeping sought way in the weedy gras:
> Her filthy parbreake all the place defiled has. (i.1.15–18)

Error's books and papers also seem animate, proliferating in ghastly confusion with the blind amphibians. The gothic horror of the encounter is exacerbated when Error's 'fruitfull cursed spawne of serpents small, / Deformed monsters, fowle, and blacke as inke' swarm and crawl all over the knight's legs, though without actually harming him. It is the very multiplicity of error that Spenser stresses here – an impossible and endless spawning that cannot be defeated. This is why so many commentators make the point that Red Cross's defeat of Error is illusory. We read this defeat as a kind of medievalist critique of earlier forms of writing that is also nostalgic for the simplicity of allegorical reading.

For Spenser, a true Protestant awakening will undo the seeming verities of the past, but the attempt to sift truth from error is made more complicated by the proliferation of texts. Indeed, Lerer draws a strong material connection between the fear of error and the textual conditions of the early printed book, another product of the Renaissance that encouraged the development of the scholarly and academic subject, in relation to the humanist recovery of the classics, to biblical scholarship and the antiquarian interest in medieval writing. While we have hinted that error can be disabling, Lerer takes a humanistic view, arguing that the fear of error is productive. He grounds the rhetoric of scholarly error in the errata sheet, which was often bound carefully into the printed book, and which became the site of 'authorial self-definition, the place where the writer poses as his own best reader, where confessions of mistake and acts of emendation establish intellectual authority'.[5] This authority could be established over matters of typesetting or doctrinal interpretation in the printing of biblical texts. The errata sheet is also 'the place where the past is publicly brought into line with the present', making 'academic life both a performance and a defense'.[6]

While the fear of error is a recognisable characteristic of all modern scholarly disciplines, Lerer suggests that Old English studies, 'perhaps more than any other modern literary discipline',

Fear, error and death

has 'the reputation as a field of right and wrong'.[7] When other languages are involved, the problems of error are compounded, as the discipline is more likely to construct its own internal hierarchies of philology and criticism, for example. These hierarchies are constructed to enable progress – and with it the humanistic narrative that encourages us to believe that we are getting closer and closer to the authentic: the real reading, the thing as it really was. Yet if these practices enable us to approach (even if asymptomatically) the past, they are also, as Lerer notes, a defence – but a defence against what?

We might get a clearer view of what the threat is by examining one of the more startling examples of the discovery and correction of error within the medieval academy. For years, scholars debated the meaning of the strange lyric known as 'How Christ Shall Come':[8]

I sayh hym wiþ ffless al bi-sprad.	He cam vram est.
I sayh hym wiþ blod al by-ssad.	He cam vram west.
I sayh þet manye he wiþ hym brouȝte.	He cam vram souȝ.
I sayh þet þe world of hym ne rouȝte.	He cam vram north.

I come vram þe wedlok as a svete spouse þet habbe my wif wiþ me inome.
I come vram viȝt, a staleworþe knyȝt, þet myne vo habbe overcome.
I come vram þe chepyng as a riche chapman þet mankynde habbe ibouȝt.
I come vram an vncouþe londe as a sely pylegrym þet ferr habbe i-souȝt.[9]

I saw him covered with flesh.	He came from the East.
I saw him drenched in blood.	He came from the West.
I saw that he brought many with him.	He came from the South.
I saw that world cared not for him.	He came from the North.

I come from wedlock as a sweet spouse who has taken my wife to wed.
I come from the fight, a stalwart knight who has overcome my foe.
I come from the market as a rich merchant who has bought mankind.
I come from an unknown land as an innocent pilgrim who has sought far.

Some thought the poem referenced the second coming of Christ.[10] Others thought that the last line referenced Christ's continuing desire to save humanity.[11] There were some doubts about metrical irregularity or flatness, but virtually all agreed that the poem was accomplished and even powerful.[12] And when it was discovered that an additional sixteen lines followed the ones above in the manuscript, much of the analysis focused on whether these extra sixteen lines belonged to this poem or a different one, as they seemed fundamentally different from the opening eight lines.

As Siegfried Wenzel put it, 'the putative problem of the poem's integrity, and indeed the other interpretative problems mentioned earlier, can be easily solved by carefully reading the context in which the stanzas occur. Such an examination reveals at once that the text in question *is not a lyrical "poem" at all*, but the formal division of a Latin sermon put into English rhyming lines.'[13] Wenzel clearly delights in his discovery and rather forcefully suggests that scholars might do well to attend to the manuscript context of medieval poems before making assertions about their literary, historical, religious or even generic qualities.[14] The story is irresistible both because it seems to demonstrate the delightful horror of academic error (as long as it doesn't happen to us) *and* demonstrates how academic discipline can keep error at bay (or at least rectify it once it has occurred).

This exemplum embodies a fantasy about the necessity of distinguishing between past and present. Like Red Cross Knight, Wenzel confronts Error (misunderstandings about the past) and seems to defeat it with disciplinary power. But in thinking further about the episode, it is less clear that the binaries governing our reception of this story (truth/error, history/subjectivity, etc.) are as stable as they appear. Were earlier critics wrong to think about these lines as poetry? There is a kind of incantatory power in a number of these lines, and their simultaneous use as a sermon mnemonic wouldn't necessarily disqualify the lines as operating like a lyric. In fact, it is their very lyric qualities that make them so useful as a mnemonic for sermons, so at the very least these lines operate analogically in terms of the lyric.[15] At most Wenzel *may* have demonstrated that these lines were not meant to be a lyric because they were meant to be understood as a mnemonic (though even here it's not clear that they were not meant to be both). But there is nothing in the form of the 'poem' to prevent a medieval audience from understanding the lines as a lyric even if that wasn't the intention of the lines' author. And it is the present reception of the language of the lines that enables us to comprehend this issue.

Even as we acknowledge how compelling this story might be for medievalists, the stakes seem relatively low. After all, our understanding of the Middle Ages will probably not hinge on whether we understand these eight or twenty-four lines as a lyric or lyrics, or sermon mnemonics, or both. Yet, as we imply above, the power of the story resides not in its content, but in its form. Error can and should be kept at bay because small scholarly errors can lead to larger, more sweeping mistakes.

In its most terrified heart, the discipline of medieval studies may even fear that popular understandings of the medieval might be perceived as sufficient in contemporary culture, rendering its hard-won expertise and pedagogical practices redundant. What if people believe, after watching Mel Gibson's *Braveheart*, that William Wallace really had a love affair with Isabella of France? Or if they think medieval people routinely burned witches and used chastity belts? But if, for a moment, we can damp down this fear, we can perceive the strange ambivalence that lies at the heart of this epistemological moment. On the one hand, it remains very clear that the language, societal structures and technology of the Middle Ages mark them out as profoundly different from contemporary culture. Indeed, one could make the argument that the Middle Ages is seen as more 'other' than classical societies. At the same time, what is popularly seen as the 'darkness' of the Middle Ages seems recognisably 'human'. This reading of the Middle Ages as ultimately mirroring contemporary society has a long history, but it was probably crystallised in the popular imagination in 1978 in the book by Barbara Tuchman that made the trope explicit by including the dark mirror of the Middle Ages in its title, *A Distant Mirror: The Calamitous Fourteenth Century*.[16]

A winner of the National Book Award in 1980, the book has remained in print for thirty-five years and shows no signs of relinquishing its place as one of the most popular books about the Middle Ages. Its title is quoted or referenced in everything from essays on medieval Islamic finance to lectures given during 'Medieval Week' – a joint venture of the British Academy and the Royal Society of Edinburgh.[17] Tuchman's history is premised on the similarities between the 'calamitous' fourteenth century – 'a violent, tormented, bewildered, suffering and disintegrating age'[18] – and the late twentieth. Such comparisons are not new. As Tuchman points out, the historian James Westfall Thompson had compared the period of the Black Death to that of World War I, citing as features shared in common by the two eras 'economic chaos, social unrest, high prices, profiteering, depraved morals, lack of production, industrial indolence, frenetic gaiety, wild expenditure, luxury, debauchery, social and religious hysteria, greed, avarice, maladministration, decay of manners'.[19] Umberto

Eco had drawn some similarly apocalyptic comparisons in 1972, drawing on a 'disturbing' book by Roberto Vacca, showing how quickly contemporary urban life could collapse in the manner of a medieval apocalypse.[20]

Tuchman comments that the fourteenth century had not been often studied because it did not seem to fit the pattern of human progress so beloved of much historiography, but 'after the experience of the terrible twentieth century, we have greater fellow-feeling for a distraught age whose rules were breaking down under the pressure of adverse and violent events'.[21] Her argument for this greater 'fellow-feeling' nevertheless rests on the idea of the historical and cultural alterity of the Middle Ages: conditions are so very different that patterns of human behaviour that we 'recognize as familiar amid these alien surroundings are revealed as permanent in human nature'.[22] The familiarity rests on a contradiction here: the past is seen as consoling in its similarities to present trauma, but it is only through great differences in social and cultural conditions that these behavioural similarities emerge.[23]

Similarly, while Tuchman draws a number of parallels between the calamitous fourteenth and twentieth centuries, she also formulates ' "Tuchman's Law": "The fact of being reported multiplies the apparent extent of any deplorable development by five- to tenfold" (or any figure the reader would care to supply).'[24] This law is applicable to both periods, but has the potential to attenuate her own claims about the exceptional similarities between the periods.

Tuchman's preface, then, cathects a number of issues for medieval studies, for medievalism studies and for the study of the history of the emotions, or affect. *A Distant Mirror* was heavily promoted and publicised, and sold many copies despite the fact that scholarly reviews were not particularly favourable. J. J. N. McGurk and Bernard S. Bachrach, for example, both imply that Tuchman is a modern specialist out of her depth in the Middle Ages: 'for a reputable modern historian who enthusiastically blundered into the fourteenth century, Barbara W. Tuchman has failed to gain a firm grasp of the world through which she rambles'.[25] McGurk comments that few specialists would be 'so amazed as the author at the gulf between the preaching and practices of medieval Christianity'.[26] Bachrach is most scornful of Tuchman's attempts to draw parallels between the fourteenth and twentieth centuries: 'Television "news" – high in the ratings but low in thought and balance – seems to have shaped her view' and oriented her 'preoccupation with lying, cheating, deceit, immorality, and high-level insanity'.[27] More recently, in a brief note, Bonnie Wheeler revisits her earlier review of *A Distant Mirror*, which she summarised as 'a really bad book … weird and warped and entirely without sympathy for its subject' and compares it to Dan Brown's *The Da Vinci Code*, arguing that both books benefited (unfairly and misleadingly, is the implication) from insistent promotion from their publishers.[28] Our point here is not so much about the snobbery associated with academic popularising culture, though that may well have played a part in the reception of Tuchman's book. Rather, we are interested in the way that all of these scholars take what Tuchman (and her readers) seem to regard as the strength of the book (the way in which the Middle Ages reflects the modern era), and attempt to demonstrate the error of promoting that pleasurable thrill of recognition by marvelling at that abjected thing: the gross alterity of the Middle Ages.

Abjection and torture

The features of this abjected medieval alterity are not hard to identify: its untreatable diseases, its rudimentary dentistry, the brutality of its warfare, its ruthless patriarchal and compulsive heterosexuality, and the repressive enforcement of its religious practices. But perhaps the most enduring conception of medieval alterity is the superstitious and brutal nature of its judicial system. From ducking (mercilessly mocked in *Monty Python and the Holy Grail*) to trial by ordeal, the means by which the medievals discerned truth have come in for special scorn. At the same time, the continuity of a practice that is insistently coded as medieval – torture – has led to the uncanny realisation that the medieval subsists within and even buttresses the modern.[29]

One of the more forthright expressions of this uncanniness that received wide distribution was an interview with Richard Bourke, an Australian lawyer who is working on behalf of the inmates at Guantanamo Bay:

> They are torturing people. They are torturing people on Guantanamo Bay. They are subjecting them to cruel and unnecessary treatment. And people sometimes argue about the definition of torture. What they're doing clearly comes within the definition of torture under the convention, under the international convention, but it also … they are engaging in acts which amount to torture in the medieval sense of the phrase. They are engaging in good old-fashioned torture, as people would have understood it in the Dark Ages.[30]

What is so telling about this quotation is the way in which Bourke moves from the definition of torture under the Geneva Convention to torture in the 'medieval sense'. His point is rhetorical, of course, as he implies that there is somehow a difference between 'medieval' torture and torture as it has been defined under the Convention. This compulsive return to the Middle Ages, even within this quotation, tells us how the idea of torture is fundamentally and essentially tied to a medieval mind-set. And ten years later, the routineness of this connection is still fuelled by the easy iterability of 'medieval' and 'torture'. For instance, Jill Lepore notes, 'Eliza Griswold, writing in *The New Republic*, quoted a former interrogator who described Bagram as echoing with "medieval sounds". The medieval dungeon: the scrape of shackles, the screams of agony, the groans of despair.'[31] It seems we have met ourselves again in the revelation that 'good old-fashioned' torture has been going on in the holding cells at Guantanamo. Bourke's phrase even suggests a kind of *heimischeness* – a sense that this is not so surprising after all, but is deeply familiar.

This persistence of torture discourse would suggest that the operative word in the various discourses concerning torture remains 'medieval' and somehow residing in that word is a thing that in its abjectness has a relationship to truth. What marks out torture as a particular test case for the relationship of medieval and modern is its relationship to epistemology. The means of working out truth in the past somehow suggests the truth of that past even as that past is used to abject the very efficacy of the truth-discerning technology. No less a figure than Sigmund Freud, in fact, suggested that those who theorised about, and used, torture in order to elicit confessions of demonic possession in the Middle Ages had real insight, even if their terminology was somewhat faulty: 'by pronouncing possession by a demon to be the cause of hysterical phenomena, the Middle Ages in fact chose this solution [the splitting of consciousness]; it would only have been a matter of exchanging the religious terminology of that dark and superstitious age for the scientific language of today'.[32] Some four years later, in 1897, Freud wrote to Wilhelm Fliess to ask,

> what would you say, by the way, if I told you that all of my brand-new prehistory of hysteria is already known and was published a hundred times over, though several centuries ago? Do you remember that I always said that the medieval theory of possession held by the ecclesiastical courts was identical with our theory of a foreign body

Fear, error and death

and the splitting of consciousness? ... Why are their confessions under torture (*auf der Folter*) so like the communications made by my patients in psychic treatment? Sometime soon I must delve into the literature on this subject.[33]

A week later Freud writes to tell him that he had purchased a copy of the fifteenth-century persecution manual, *Malleus Maleficarum* (Hammer of the Witches), and that he could now understand 'the harsh therapy of the witches' judges'.[34] Here is Freud's own moment of abjection in which he at once wishes to distance himself from what he characterises in familiar terms as a 'dark and superstitious age' even as he recognises the similarities – indeed, the helpful analogies – between the inquisitors of the medieval period and his own psychoanalytic method.[35] At stake in the analogy is the ability to deal with the split in consciousness – the ability to bring repressed memories into the conscious mind. In terms of the medieval inquisitors, this involves uncovering and having the subject confess that they are possessed; in terms of psychoanalytic techniques, to have the patient admit to thoughts that he or she had repressed.[36]

The timing of this interest in torture and the analogy between the medieval inquisitors and psychoanalysts is telling. For in the same year that Freud wrote to Fliess in order to suggest the applicability of the inquisitorial model to psychoanalysis, he famously altered his idea about what lay behind neurosis.[37] No longer would he claim that the etiology of disease included historical instances of childhood seduction; rather these instances were imagined, or, as he would later say, unconscious libidinal fantasies. In other words, within eight months of suggesting that there was not so much difference between medieval torturers and nineteenth-century analysts, Freud fundamentally altered his own relationship to the ability to recover history. Repressed memories could no longer be trusted to refer to events that had a historical reality. Instead, these memories were signs of fantasies that had themselves been repressed. It is not too much, we think, to claim that the Middle Ages was one of the stumbling blocks that led Freud to distance himself from the idea that all repressed memories necessarily referred to actual historical events.[38] In order to make sense of the fact that 'their confessions under torture [were] so like the communications made by my patients in psychic treatment',[39] he had to imagine that the confessions of the medieval victims (sex with the devil, flying on brooms) were already a displaced version of these victims' histories. The devil in this instance must have been someone who was disguised, while 'flying' on a 'broomstick' is a metaphor for intercourse. And, in fact, later in the second letter to Fliess where he talks about witches he seems to foreshadow his move to fantasy when he argues that it is form not content that is ultimately crucial: 'perverse actions, moreover, are always the same – meaningful and fashioned according to some pattern that someday will be understood'.[40] Freud's formal move, then, is to suggest that it is the confession, not the historical event behind the confession, that carries meaning.

Put this way, Freud's own relationship to the Middle Ages is encompassed both by what we have called the 'medieval' and 'medievalism'. He believed, for a time, that the confessions made under torture, like the memories uncovered by people like Charcot and Fliess, were historically true. And, indeed, he would later wax nostalgic about the uncomplicated time before this crucial change when it seemed possible to recover past history unproblematically. Finally, however, he was forced to realise that these recovered memories were not always true. Both his inability to carry out a single successful analysis and the sheer unlikelihood that so many 'perversions against children' had been carried out were two of the reasons that he gives for abandoning his earlier theory. But theoretically crucial to our project is the third reason that he gave: 'the certain insight that there are no indications of reality in the unconscious, so that one cannot distinguish between truth and fiction that has been cathected with affect'.[41] What we would like to suggest here is that Freud's understanding of his patients' personal histories recapitulated his own understanding of the Middle Ages. Just as he was forced to admit that his own notion of these histories was a kind of creation of the patients themselves rather than any 'real' verifiable historical event, so too his understanding of the 'confessions' wrung from the victims of medieval torture also turned out to be a fantasy. Hence his view of the medieval (itself dependent on the fantasies that were taken from those victims) was a kind of fantasy. In his own words, 'I dream, therefore, of a primeval devil religion with rites that are carried on secretly, and understand the harsh therapy of the witches' judges. Connecting links abound.'[42] In his dream, he creates a secret origin that he may uncover with the aid of his method. At this moment, he confesses that the 'facts' that he supposedly marshals in order to demonstrate the efficacy of his method are actually the product of the dream world of the unconscious.

Suggestively enough, Freud had another dream shortly after meeting Fliess in Nuremburg where he apparently encountered some resistance to his enthusiasm for the Middle Ages.[43] In a letter, he says 'you were unable to take any pleasure at all in the Middle Ages ... thus the dream brings together all the annoyance with you that is unconsciously present in me'.[44] We might wish to be careful about projecting our own fantasies onto Freud's dream. But we can see why Fliess would have problems equating their methods with those of medieval inquisitors. And, indeed, Freud himself might well be unconsciously expressing discomfort with his own secret pleasure in the more sanguinary aspects of the Middle Ages. The slippage between truth discernment, punishment and pleasure here suggests that we might frame the question about the Middle Ages and abjection in a slightly different way. It is not whether the Middle Ages is necessarily always abject; it is whether the abjection we feel is a way at getting at the truth. In Freud's case, he found himself in the familiarly uncomfortable position analogous to that of the medieval torturer – one who allegedly wishes to get at the truth, but instead finds himself taking pleasure in the abjectness of the Middle Ages.

Abjecting the abjected

This abjection might seem removed from Julia Kristeva's influential formulation of the abjection of bodily excess – the way that bodily fluids and waste blur the boundaries of inside and outside and make manifest fears and anxieties about the borders of the self. But we propose that there is something like a form of cultural or historical abjection in the relations between modernity and the Middle Ages that is comparable. Contemplation of this form of historical abjection also presents itself as an emotional relationship to the past.

As noted above, there are many familiar and possible routes to the abjected past. Much medieval cinema thrives on these features: on mist, mud, tortured and leprous bodies, sexual and ethnic violence and an apparent disregard for individual human life. The dominance of the cinematic medium further encourages us to see the Middle Ages as radically other: from the comfort of our cinema seats or our own lounge rooms, we can reflect on the appalling brutality of this other world, presented primarily through the lens of the fantastic rather than the historical other, as many commentators have argued.[45]

That is, despite the gruesome and fearful depiction of the Middle Ages, its coding as fantasy actually *limits* the production of the affective response, because it presents such a clear distinction between – if not then and now – between them and us. In contrast, a number of medieval texts specifically *invite* an affective response, in ways that continue to blur the distinction between subject and object, between text and reader. This is particularly the case with the spiritual enthusiasms and the mortifications of the flesh that are such a dramatic feature of late medieval affective piety. These modes of religious expression are both distinctly medieval, but also recognisable in some forms of Western and Eastern asceticism. So, for example, acts of self-flagellation are regularly offered up as dramatic, and sometimes parodic, contrasts to modern, enlightened sensibility, from the *The Seventh Seal* to *Monty Python and the Holy Grail*, *The Name of the Rose* and *The Da Vinci Code*. But medieval practices such as food denial are sometimes construed as recognisable historical antecedents of modern pathologies.[46]

Some of the most famous instances are found in the lives of Catherine of Siena and Angela of Foligno. Caroline Walker Bynum has drawn analogies between Catherine's devotional practices that were centred around the provision and consumption, as well as the non-consumption and regurgitation, of food and modern anorectic or bulimic illness.[47] But of all Catherine's ascetic testing, we are most struck by her care of the older Sister Andrea, who was sick with breast cancer, whose 'whole breast became a mass of corruption'.[48] Catherine nurses her when all have abandoned her because of the stench, until one day the devil tests her. As she uncovers the ulcer one day, a 'more than usually disgusting odour arose from it'. Catherine is on the point of vomiting, but turns on herself:

> 'Are you disgusted,' she said, 'with a Sister of your own, redeemed in the Blood of the Saviour, you who may well end up yourself by falling into the same malady, or a worse one? As the Lord lives, you will be punished for your fault.'[49]

And on this she pressed her mouth and nose into the cancerous flesh until she had subdued her own revulsion. A second time, after other events (in which this woman spread malicious sexual rumours about Catherine), the devil once more produces a feeling of revulsion, and again Catherine turns on herself:

'As the Lord lives, who is the beloved Spouse of my soul, you will be made to swallow down the thing for which you show such deep disgust.' So saying, she gathered into a bowl the water with which the ulcer had been washed and the corrupt matter which had come away with it, and going to one side she swallowed it. On the instant, all feeling of disgust died down within her.[50]

She later commented, 'Never since the day I was born did any food or drink I ever took afford me such sweetness and delight'.[51]

This example is frequently cited, and clustered with similar acts of self-abnegation.[52] We draw attention here to the gag reflex that Catherine masters, as it is such a dramatic example of psychological and emotional mastery over the primary fear of the 'corrupt matter' of the diseased breast, the abjection of bodily waste and decay of which Kristeva writes. This episode rarely fails to produce a similar gag reflex in readers or students hearing it for the first time. Catherine draws strength from her own sisterhood with this afflicted woman, when she addresses herself, 'you who may well end up yourself by falling into the same malady, or a worse one'.

This episode is less often examined as part of the history of breast cancer, a disease that is sometimes said to be a particular affliction of modern industrialised society. It is also a disease that continues to strike fear into modern women, in a society obsessed with female appearance and sexuality as defining characteristics of womanhood. But modern cancers, in the West, at least, rarely progress to the stage of ulcerating sores: breast cancer is one of the most high-profile, heavily funded 'popular' diseases of the twenty-first century, with high levels of attentive remedial medical care. Catherine's account, then, brings us that much closer to the medieval medical body: the site of its own horror; and a typical indicator, like medieval dentistry, of why we would not want to live in the medieval past.

It would be foolish to deny this separation, but we would argue that it is also foolish to deny the ways in which the abject links us to the past. In speaking of the ways in which empathic connections are formed, Michael Eigen insists on the need to embrace what he calls the annihilated self. As he puts it:

> We dream of fear of dying, corpses, threatening figures. Corpses come to life, creaking, trying to move with rusty hinges. Deadspots. Killers and rapists threaten to overpower us in dreams. Fear of being overpowered permeates psychic life. I don't think any of us survive infancy or childhood fully alive. What lives survives on graves of

self that didn't make it. We leave a lot behind to be what we are now, to be what we can be. We cover not only nakedness but annihilation. We try to look better than we are, more alive, more appealing. We try to mask a sense of an annihilated self with signs of life.[53]

Our psychic past is marked by all of those things that we have rejected and, understandably, we hide or repress them, identifying them in dreams with all that is abject (dead things, mutilations, blood). At the same time, there is an understanding that what we abject, attempt to hide or expel makes up a part of ourselves no matter how much we mask it. And Eigen argues we simultaneously find this part of our self revolting, and need to reach this part of our 'real' annihilated selves. At its most dangerous, this drive to reach 'the realness of our annihilated beings' can lead us to injure or destroy others, as we re-enact rather than remember and reveal them. This is the cruelty of the torturers who project onto others the things that they see in themselves. This is an attempt to abject what is already abjected and is doomed to failure.

Catherine, on the other hand, embraces the abject breast, at once projecting herself into futurity, but also signalling that she recognises already within herself that which is dead. It is, of course, the well-recognised genius of Christianity to take the abject and make it sublime, chiasmatically to make the dead alive, the first last. To take just one example, as spiritual reward Catherine is granted a vision in which Christ draws her to the wound in his side and invites her to drink his blood: 'Drawn close ... to the outlet of the Fountain of Life, she fastened her lips upon that sacred wound, and still more eagerly the mouth of her soul, and there she slaked her mystic thirst for long and long.'[54] Again, such spiritual feasting can be explained, rationalised and historicised according to medieval practices of affective piety (and we note here the text's insistence on the spiritual over the physical – even in the visionary state ['still more eagerly the mouth of her soul']) – but the shock of the vampiric moment persists here as a trace of the abject, and of the abjected past.

So how does this present abjection link us with the past? Certainly, it signals a kind of understanding of primary feelings such as pain and disgust as somehow atavistic, something that enables us (as Freud suggests) to connect with the primeval. As Eigen puts it, 'pain resonates, links'.[55] Catherine felt it for her sister, and we feel it through her words. And so, as we feel the pain, shame and abjection of others, this enables us to connect through negative affect with the past. But more disturbingly, we also feel connections, we argue, with those who are responsible for pain. Certainly, Freud's sympathy with the inquisitors comes to mind here, but also the pleasure we take in the touristy commodification of medieval pain. On the one hand, the 'harsh methods' of the witch's judges are 'understood' and 'connecting links abound'. On the other hand, the denatured, late modern medievalist spectacle of torture is somehow made safe by its very recreational character even as it relies on its connection to the medieval.

If we turn this understanding back onto a well-known medieval text that has everything to do with pain, abjection and shame, *The Book of Margery Kempe*, we see that it opens up an alternative understanding of how a reader can interact with the text. Anyone who has taught the work knows all too well how quickly students can subject Kempe to modernist scrutiny, categorise her as a hysteric, dismiss her text as obsessive, her revelations as post-natal psychosis, her behaviour as aberrant. The solution that many of us employ is to normalise her 'pathology' or to contextualise it, by situating her food practices in relation to the lives of other European visionaries, mystics or ascetics, as indeed Kempe does in her frequent comparison of herself with St Bridget of Sweden.

But there are times in the text when Margery herself seems to have self-awareness about how her own abjectness distances her from others. She attempts to control the uncontrollable and fit into the normalised role that society has constructed for her:

> And therfor, whan sche knew that sche schulde cryen, sche kept it in as long as sche mygth and dede al that sche cowde to withstond it er ellys to put it awey, til sche wex as blo as any leed, and evyr it schuld labowryn in hir mende mor and mor into the tyme that it broke owte. And, whan the body myth ne lengar enduryn the gostly labowr, but was ovyrcome wyth the unspekabyl lofe that wrowt so fervently in the sowle, than fel sche down and cryed wondyr lowde. And the mor that sche wolde labowryn to kepe it in er to put it awey, mech the mor schulde sche cryen and the mor lowder. And thus sche dede in the Mownt of Calvarye, as it is wretyn beforn.[56]

Margery's struggle for self-control is a form of emotional work against the addiction of crying that is recognisable to modern audiences, even if the concept of the 'unspeakable love of God' is less familiar. Carolyn Dinshaw writes about the connections, the queer touches that might hold Kempe, Hope Emily Allen and Dinshaw herself together across time and place.[57] The recognition of emotional feeling is another such affective thread, even when Kempe's religious sensibility seems so abnormal and irregular.

However, in our experience, such moments of emotional recognition are never straightforward or static: they tend to be played out dialectically with a pleasurable shared horror at the excesses of Margery's shouting and weeping, her strange sexual bargains with her husband, and so forth. And so it seems to us that one of the strategies of the text is to, at times, put us in the position of those who would abject Margery. For it is only through this understanding of the abject that we can come to any appreciation of how Margery's actions can be seen as truly alternative. To completely historicise, normalise, queer or abject Margery seems to understate the extent to which the text dynamically engages its audience through the push me/pull you of abjection.

With Catherine and Margery, this embrace of abjection leads, as Lochrie has argued, to the sublime. From our point of view, this chiasmic understanding of the world enables the sure knowledge that to conquer death one only needs to die. But the hope held out by the Christian promise of immortality to medieval readers is not as readily available to contemporary readers of medieval texts. In fact, the disjunction between Christian hope and contemporary despair is often the topic of medievalist renderings of the confrontation with death. So how do we square this insistence on dissimilarity with our argument that the medieval and the medievalist are in some sense continuous? We suggest that medievalist meditations on death are less about how one can reach back into the Middle Ages and more about how the Middle Ages reaches out morbidly to us.

Playing for time

With all this talk of death and despair it is legitimate to ask: are we doomed to rely on all of this negative affect in order to survive? The frisson of the abject might seem a tactical way to pique contemporary interest in the Middle Ages, but as a long-term strategy we wonder if such a deathly hermeneutic might not hasten our own extinction. We don't counsel turning away from death (to do so would be as futile as it would be dishonest); instead we turn to the ways in which inviting the morbid embrace of the Middle Ages is not a dead end, but a dialectic between death and futurity that characterises medievalism. We turn to one of the most famous cinematic treatments of death, Ingmar Bergman's *The Seventh Seal* (1957), as a meditation on the dialogic relationship of death and futurity that contains not the promise of immortality, but the potential for hope.

It would be hard, indeed, to overestimate the influence of *The Seventh Seal* on subsequent cinematic versions of the medieval.[58] So many of its key scenes and encounters have become stock features of medieval film: the knight returning from the Crusades; the game of chess; the fear of plague; the flagellants; the travelling players, etc. Yet the discursive direction of the film sits in tension with the ways these visual scenes are customarily interpreted and represented. Bergman's film shows the Middle Ages at odds with itself, as it were, presenting a variety of responses to death. Most notably, Bergman's knight, Block, never expresses the panic and fear of sufferers in Last Judgment scenes, and his fear is not of Death, who is similarly depicted in calm humour. Nickolas Haydock characterises this aspect of the film:

> Block's confession is a litany of postwar existential emptiness: 'my heart is a void, the void is a mirror, I look at myself and feel loathing and terror.' The mise-en-scène replicates the mirror structures of medieval *memento mori*, on the other side of the mirror-screen is the void of death into which the knight pours his deepest fears and in which he finally sees the image of his own future change from opaque to liquid as Death turns to face him.[59]

As Haydock shows, the knight Block, playing chess with Death, seems a strikingly modern figure:

> Block's situation at the border of sea and shore marks a kind of midpoint in his transition between a genocidal holocaust (the Crusades) and the threat of an apocalypse (the Black Death), analogous perhaps to Bergman's own situation in 1957 between World War II and the prospect of all-out nuclear war.[60]

The Seventh Seal does not so much meditate on the abjection of death as project an impossible futurity. Unlike Tuchman's distant mirror that reflects our own relationship to a medievalist negative affect, the film locates the mirror at the heart of the medieval so that the medieval can meditate upon itself. What the medieval sees is self-loathing and terror. What modernity sees is its own troubled relationship with time and meaning. The only thing that is certain about the future is that at some point there will be no future, and for the knight this creates a problem because he believes that it is only in the future that significance can be found.

Crucially, and in terms that are now familiar, the knight bewails his lack of epistemological certainty, saying that what he wants is 'knowledge (*vetskap*). Not belief. Not assumptions. But knowledge.'[61] Block characterises what has generally been taken as the lesson of the movie when he says, 'My whole life has been a meaningless search... I say it without bitterness or self-reproach.'[62] What he says he desires most is that God will no longer be a product of interpretation or faith, but will finally reveal himself. But as he nears his end, and bargains with death for more life, he says something a bit different, 'I want to use my respite for one significant action'.[63]

This action (knocking over the chessboard) at the end of the film, enables a family to slip away from Death (distracted as he is by picking up the chess pieces). The significance of Block's action is that he is able to grant futurity to others even if, in the terms of the game, the knight must sacrifice himself. This logic of self-sacrifice and the meaning it provides can certainly be read as a kind of Christian hope where meaning might be insistently deferred to the future. Significance is realised for one's self only in the ability to defer an end that might lead to meaninglessness. And the fear is that Death will intervene before we can inscribe meaning into our life. Significantly, the delay that enables Block this meaning is based on his ability to know – not God – but something about Death (his interest in chess). When Death asks Block how he knows, he says that he has seen it in paintings and heard it sung in ballads, a comment that suggests a connection between epistemology and artistic representation that might well appeal to a director who is making a film about a medieval knight's desire to 'know'.

This connection becomes even more apparent when we consider the enduring image of the final scene in the film, the dance of death. What is most apparent about this scene is its difference from 'authentically medieval' dances of death. As Seeta Chaganti points out, 'unlike the iconic modern depiction of the dance of death at the end of Ingmar Bergman's *The Seventh Seal* (1957), which takes place on an empty hilltop with a background of clouds, many medieval dances of death use the imagery of buildings and architecture to organize their visual information'.[64] It is worth remembering that this is the *second* representation of the dance in the film. In an earlier scene, Block's squire, Jöns, has a long conversation with a 'pictor' in a church who, in front of his depiction of the dance of death, says that he paints the grotesqueness of the dance in order to frighten people and that this is a representation of 'things as they are'.[65] This matter-of-fact evocation of *memento mori* seems to dovetail with Haydock's interpretation of the film's desire to mirror the Middle Ages – to show things as they really were. And the preoccupation with the more grisly aspects of death seems to reflect a Huizinga-like medievalism that represents late

Fear, error and death

medieval art and literature as coarsened by the morbidity and malaise that attended post-plague society.⁶⁶ Yet the final vision of the dance is an aesthetic *tour de force* that belies this reading. Freed from stasis and the claustrophobic and dark interior of the church, the actual dance is seen by the audience only through the eyes of Jof, whose ability to see visions gives him a special ability to 'know'. The final words of Jof's wife, Mia, 'You with your dreams and visions' (*drömmar och syner*), suggests at once the oneiric quality of that which we have just seen and the possibility of a different way of seeing that is available only through the cinema.⁶⁷

In its own way, too, medieval literature dramatises the fear of death in a way that aids a form of temporal pleating between past and present, through the tropes of *memento mori* and the *ubi sunt* formulae. These tropes mobilise the backwards look in the service of an eschatological future. The past in all its glory has disappeared; and the future promises to do the same. The Latin phrase *timor mortis conturbat me*, 'the fear of death confounds me', is often quoted in this context, lifted out of the Office of the Dead and used as the refrain in a number of macaronic poems that mediate its Latinity for a vernacular, often more personalised, audience. The phrase uses the present tense to dramatise the perpetual state of terror, or paralysis, induced by the fear of death. The pleasure of the Latin citation works to frame and control this emotion. Quoting and reading it, we can align ourselves in comfortable proximity with the medieval past, without the distraction of plague buboes or the insidious creep of worms and snakes into the corpse. Just as the familiar ritual of ecclesiastical repetition brings comfort, so too does the repeated tradition of this citation. In Dunbar's 'Lament for the makirs', the Latin refrain rhymes with the third line of each of the twenty-five stanzas:

> I that in heill (health) was and gladnèss
> Am trublit now with great sickness
> And feblit with infirmitie: –
> *Timor Mortis conturbat me*⁶⁸

The penultimate stanza rehearses the lesson that extends back into the past of the poet, which is also our own past, too, with its relentless logic and deathly conclusion: death comes to us all,

> Sen (since) he has all my brether tane (taken),
> He will naught let me live alane;
> Of force (necessity) I man (must) his next prey be: –
> *Timor Mortis conturbat me*⁶⁹

In another fifteenth-century poem with the same refrain, the poet heads out in a merry morning, but encounters a bird who both weeps and sings of the 'dread of death', a fear that is presented as a universal gloss on a spring morning:

> Whan I shal deye, I knowe no day,
> What contree or place I can not seye;
> Wher-fore this song synge I may –
> *Timor mortis conturbat me.*[70]

This poem's rhetoric is tied even less securely than Dunbar's to place, country or, we may say, to time. Even Christ shares the bird's fears:

> Jhesu Crist, whan he sholde deye,
> To his Fader he gan seye,
> 'Fader,' he seyde, 'in trinitee,
> *Timor mortis conturbat me.*[71]

The fear of death, then – thanataphobia – is intimately bound up with the spiritual and ethical rhetoric of these poems. This universal condition, fear of imminent death, repeatable after every three-line summary of every human condition, is even used as a marker for the significance of the ultimate sacrifice – a sign that for action to be meaningful there can be no certitude.

This fear is privileged insofar as it becomes a symptom of the desire for meaning and the only way to ensure that meaning is to project into the future. Block's action at the end of *The Seventh Seal* ensures continuation for the family, a continuation that is often read as an allegorical reaching back for the Holy Family whose own survival ensures our own continuation and freedom from death.[72] This endless deferral of meaning has, of course, come in for criticism. As a 'fantasy of meaning that futurism constantly weaves' it sustains 'the subject's relation to the reproduction of meaning'.[73] The path towards meaning here is a straight one, aiming towards an ideological wholeness promised by meaning that is only available insofar as we reproduce the past in the future. Lee Edelman argues that to the extent that a non-continuative approach to time poses a threat to such meaning, it actually reinforces or enables the continuation of meaning. The fear is the fear of death but also of the death drive that seems to eliminate the possibility of reproductive futurity and thus disrupts our attempt to straighten out time.

The perpetual threat of death in these poems allows us, nevertheless, to control its disappearance and reappearance. In this regard, it bears a close analogy with the *fort-da* game of medievalist cinema in the analysis of Haydock, for whom 'movie medievalism ... is as much about making the past gone as it is about the endlessly renewable surprises inherent in finding it again'.[74] As we play for/with time, we offer ourselves a form of futurity, while each loss anticipates the thrill of finding. But we don't just *find* the medieval again; we revive it, and not just in cinematic form. And by revival, we do not mean simply, or not alone, the metaphor by which we re-enact or rehearse the medieval past. Nor do we mean simply the dramatic revival of the dead or dying that belongs to the trope of speaking with the past. Instead, we mean this dreadful tension between past, present and future in a kind of necromancy of which we will speak further in chapter 4.[75]

On the one hand, then, we need to embrace death, not only our own, but the death that necessarily conditions history. All books, as D. Vance Smith reminds us, in some sense connote the death of the work.[76] They are the endpoint, the formal crystallisation of a work's innate form. They are the only things left to us to interpret and understand the period that we study. But from our point of view they are the beginning of understanding the work, not the end. In fact, it's possible for the formal characteristics of the book to do injury to the work itself (as Smith argues). The hope that we hold out is not that we can reproduce medieval meaning, but that we can revive it. What too often holds us back is fear of error, the desire to get it right. But like Red Cross Knight, we sometimes become so rigid in our attempt to identify and defeat Error that we ourselves err – mistaking the means of understanding for the thing itself.

Notes

1. There are many other matters of concern to medievalists, of course: not least our interest in ensuring our communities are sensitive to issues of race, sexual and gender identity, disability and the increasing casualisation of our profession.
2. Patterson, 'On the margin', p. 102.
3. Lerer, *Error and the Academic Self*.
4. All quotations from *The Faerie Queene* are cited in text by book, canto and stanza.
5. Lerer, *Error and the Academic Self*, p. 2.
6. Lerer, *Error and the Academic Self*, p. 17.
7. Lerer, *Error and the Academic Self*, p. 55.
8. First published by Brown (ed.), *Religious Lyrics*, pp. 52–3.
9. The text is taken from Wenzel, 'Poets, preachers', p. 343.

10 Manning, *Wisdom and Number*, pp. 19–21.
11 Reiss, *The Art of the Middle English Lyric*, p. 117.
12 One notable exception was Kane, *Middle English Literature*, p. 157.
13 Wenzel, 'Poets, preachers', p. 345, emphasis in original.
14 The lines here are uniquely present in Oxford, Merton College, MS 248, which contains a large number of Latin sermons collected by the Benedictine monk John Sheppey.
15 In fact, Wenzel comes close to acknowledging as much in a curious defence of the language of these lines being understood as lyrical ('Poets, preachers', p. 351).
16 Tuchman, *A Distant Mirror*.
17 Maidment, 'Islamic finance'; Caie and Jones, 'The Middle Ages, a distant mirror'.
18 Tuchman, *A Distant Mirror*, p. xv.
19 Tuchman, *A Distant Mirror*, p. xvi.
20 Eco, 'Towards a new Middle Ages', pp. 488–504. It should be noted, though, that Eco was less interested in simple historical comparison between the medieval and the modern (which 'has all the look of a pointless joke') than in constructing a kind of 'hypothesis of the medieval': what conditions would need to be in place if we were to produce 'an effective and plausible' Middle Ages ('Towards a new Middle Ages', p. 490).
21 Tuchman, *A Distant Mirror*, p. xvi.
22 Tuchman, *A Distant Mirror*, p. xvi.
23 We would also wish to acknowledge that there is a degree of occlusion of cultural and ethnic differences in the affirmation of 'familiar' or 'permanent' patterns of human behaviour: the perspective here is strictly Eurocentric and diachronic.
24 Tuchman, *A Distant Mirror*, p. xviii.
25 Bachrach, '*A Distant Mirror*', p. 724.
26 McGurk, '*A Distant Mirror*', p. 412.
27 Bachrach, '*A Distant Mirror*', p. 724.
28 Wheeler, 'Medieval marketing', p. 12.
29 Even more galling for some scholars is the extent to which the ficticity of this abject world so often hides in plain sight. We need only think of the pleasurable thrill that one might find in any number of 'medieval' castles that are open for tourists to visit. For instance, 'inside the walled medieval Carcassonne castle, filled with Middle Age props [sic] and the feigned sounds of a torture chamber, children joust like knights, dress in valiant armour and revel in the magic of the fortress setting' (www.cnn.com/2003/TRAVEL/DESTINATIONS/09/29/sprj.ft03.carcassonne/, accessed 20 June 2017). So too, The Museum of Medieval Torture Instruments in Prague offers 'a gaudy tribute to pain that features screaming wax figures stretched on the rack. The torture displays are accompanied by an exhibition of live spiders and scorpions' (www.prague.tv/zine/article.php?name=sexmuseum, accessed 20 June

2017). Torture can be a touristy spectacle that is domesticated precisely because it is a recreation – something that exists among children who dress up and needs the added attraction of 'live spiders and scorpions' to raise the hackles on the back of one's neck. As a playful recreation, medievalism makes manifest its recreational nature *and* works to link this explicitly false Middle Ages to the so-called 'real' Middle Ages.

30 The quotation is taken from the transcript of an interview conducted by Linda Mottram from the Australian Broadcasting Corporation's radio programme, AM. The programme aired on Wednesday, 8 October 2003.
31 Lepore, 'The dark ages', p. 30.
32 The occasion for this speculation was the death of Jean-Martin Charcot, for whom Freud wrote an obituary (Freud, *The Standard Edition*, vol. 3, p. 20).
33 Freud, *The Complete Letters*, p. 224.
34 Freud, *The Complete Letters*, p. 227.
35 In her analysis of the *Malleus Maleficarum* and epistemology, Kathleen Biddick refers briefly to Freud's ownership of the book (*The Shock of Medievalism*, pp. 116–17).
36 Alexander Doty and Patricia Ingham also deal with Freud's interest in this material and his medievalism, although their argument focuses more on the figure of the witch than the practice of torture – perhaps inevitable as their focus is Benjamin Christian's great film *Häxan*; in English, literally 'The Witch' (*The Witch and the Hysteric*, pp. 31–41).
37 He 'confides ... the great secret' to Fliess in a letter dated 21 September 1897 (Freud, *The Complete Letters*, pp. 264–6).
38 Critics like Peter Swales have seen Freud's interest in the medieval as compromising his epistemological claims ('A fascination with witches', pp. 21–5). For a critique of this position and a more nuanced treatment of the role of fantasy in psychoanalysis, see Doty and Ingham, *The Witch and the Hysteric*, pp. 34–9.
39 Freud, *The Complete Letters*, p. 224.
40 Freud, *The Complete Letters*, p. 227.
41 Freud, *The Complete Letters*, p. 264.
42 Freud, *The Complete Letters*, p. 227.
43 The meeting took place on 16–18 April 1897. The letter is dated 28 April.
44 Freud, *The Complete Letters*, p. 236.
45 See, for instance, Bildhauer, *Filming the Middle Ages*, pp. 8–9; Doty and Ingham, *The Witch and the Hysteric*, passim.
46 The most notable example is Rudolph Bell's *Holy Anorexia*, a book that generated such sharp disagreements that one journal published two conflicting reviews (Valentine and Rabuzzi, '*Holy Anorexia* (review)', pp. 167–70.
47 Bynum, *Holy Feast and Holy Fast*, particularly pp. 165–82.
48 Raymond of Capua, *Life of Catherine of Siena*, p. 147.

49 Raymond of Capua, *Life of Catherine of Siena*, p. 149.
50 Raymond of Capua, *Life of Catherine of Siena*, p. 148.
51 Raymond of Capua, *Life of Catherine of Siena*, p. 149.
52 See, for instance, Karma Lochrie, who reads this episode as the moment when Catherine is able 'to topple abjection into the sublime' (*Margery Kempe*, p. 41).
53 Eigen, 'The annihilated self', p. 25.
54 Raymond of Capua, *Life of Catherine of Siena*, p. 156. Raymond repeatedly, even obsessively, uses forms of the word *abominare* (which Kearns translates as 'disgust').
55 Eigen, 'The annihilated self', p. 29.
56 *The Book of Margery Kempe*, pp. 165–6.
57 Dinshaw, *How Soon Is Now?*, p. 121.
58 Bildhauer asserts that this film is not only canonical, but actually acts as a reference point for other 'medieval' films (*Filming the Middle Ages*, p. 13).
59 Haydock, *Movie Medievalism*, p. 43.
60 Haydock, *Movie Medievalism*, p. 41.
61 Bergman (dir.), *Seventh Seal*.
62 Bergman (dir.), *Seventh Seal*.
63 Bergman (dir.), *Seventh Seal*.
64 Chaganti, '*Danse macabre*', pp. 16–17.
65 Bergman (dir.), *Seventh Seal*.
66 Johan Huizinga's well-known account of death and the *danse macabre* has been largely superseded by more nuanced treatments (*Waning of the Middle Ages*, pp. 124–35). See, for instance, Paul Binski, who argues against the idea of cultural causations of art (*Medieval Death*, pp. 126–34). For a bibliography of critiques of Huizinga's treatment of death, see Kinch, *Imago Mortis*, p. 4, n. 9.
67 Bergman (dir.), *Seventh Seal*.
68 Dunbar, 'Lament for the makirs', pp. 316–18, lines 1–4.
69 Dunbar, 'Lament for the makirs', pp. 316–18, lines 93–5.
70 Stevick (ed.), *One Hundred Middle English Lyrics*, p. 135, lines 9–12.
71 Stevick (ed.), *One Hundred Middle English Lyrics*, p. 135, lines 13–16.
72 The parents' names are Jos and Mia (Joseph and Mary). William F. Woods remarks that 'they are the remnant, the embodiment of our eternal hope for the future' (*The Medieval Filmscape*, p. 79).
73 Edelman, *No Future*, p. 113.
74 Haydock, *Movie Medievalism*, p. 5.
75 In a suggestive, if brief, discussion of *The Seventh Seal*, Bildhauer argues that the film blurs the line between life and death. The dead seem to be alive and the alive dead. Past and future are co-present and thus there is no escape into the past (*Filming the Middle Ages*, pp. 64–5).
76 Smith, 'The inhumane wonder of the book', p. 362.

4
Loving the past

> ... what you end up remembering isn't always the same as what you have witnessed.
>
> Julian Barnes[1]

When we first began writing to and speaking with each other about the relationship between the medieval and medievalism, it was apparent that even as medievalism was gaining acceptance as a serious object of study, medieval studies had gone into something of a defensive crouch – insisting on and even policing its own disciplinary boundaries; if not in print, then certainly in informal, anecdotal contexts, in appointment practices and in the unspoken assumptions of the university syllabus. The reason for this insistence on discipline, we argued in 2008, was that (in terms already sketched out by John Guillory though in a different context), 'the difficulty in understanding medieval texts had to be maintained in the face of the popular medievalist reception of such texts' because otherwise there would be no justification for maintaining a master class of scholars who disseminated this cultural capital. Hence popular recuperations of the medieval were characterised as misunderstandings – 'a kind of afterbirth which maintained only an attenuated relationship to the real work of medieval studies'.[2] We argued that this retreat to the disciplined space was, in fact, a mistake and that we needed to get over the embarrassment of practising medievalism. We might, we said, have 'to read contemporary medievalist fantasy fiction and take it seriously, or we might have to dress up in a velvet robe, weave our own baskets or fight each other with rattan swords before an audience of enthusiasts'.[3] Time has moved on since we wrote those words, and we recognise an increasing variety of medievalist practices. And while not all medievalists have donned velvet robes, it no longer seems quite so embarrassing to so many to suggest that one might.

In fact, things have changed so dramatically that where those involved in medieval studies once worked to keep that discipline separate from medievalism, there are some who study medievalism (as we discussed earlier) who are now working to separate themselves from the medieval. Yet both separatist groups and both impulses rely on an old but persistent myth of medievalism – that it is simply a kind of screen upon which contemporary fantasies of the past are projected.[4] As Umberto Eco describes it, 'there is no real interest in the historical background; the Middle Ages are taken as a sort of mythological stage on which to place contemporary characters'.[5] The Middle Ages created by medievalism in this model is always 'fake' or 'ersatz'.[6] It tells us a lot about the eras that create specific medievalist 'fantasies', because these fantasies are the creation of passionate minds that inhabit that age. The work of uncovering the Middle Ages, so the story goes, is left to critical medieval studies which *dis*passionately pores over the surviving material culture of the past in order to conjure a more or less accurate representation of medieval history. The media for critical medieval studies are the leftovers of the Middle Ages – the succession of manuscripts, buildings and material objects; while the proper method for interpreting these remains is the theoretical and historical rigour obtained through training. Medievalism, on the other hand, seems to have no medium. It is a recreation that might be based on the remains of the Middle Ages, but it is ultimately divorced both from the fragments of the past and the ambition to cobble together these fragments into something approximating what was.

Given that so much work has been done on the complex relationship of medievalism to the past, why does this myth of medievalism's disconnection from the past persist? In part it is a function of the split between practitioners of medievalism who often claim there is a historical kernel to their projections, and the ideological, academic critique of such practices. But it is also because the nature of the medium of medievalism remains undefined. After all, if medievalism is not simply a presentist projection of a fantasy of the past, but can actually lay claim to a connection with the past, that connection will be subtle, ambivalent and mutable and will thus resist the easy narratives of modernist appropriation. As we will see, any attempt to understand the connection between medievalism and the Middle Ages is contingent on two other related questions. What is the nature of the connection of critical medieval studies to the past? And how does that connection differ from the connection to which medievalism, at times quite capriciously, and from a range of different perspectives, lays claim?

We take as our point of departure in this section recent discussions about the importance of affect to literary study. Epistemological and ontological questions give way, in this chapter, to affective ones. Specifically, we begin with the ways in which love for the past has coloured the formation of medieval literary studies. The received narrative is based on a series of binaries. Initially an enthusiasm that supported and justified the study of the medieval, love for the past became abjected with the professionalism of literary studies as an embarrassing sign of amateurism. As a result, the world of medieval studies was divided between those who valued enlightenment thinking and reason and those who relied on antiquarian models of passion.[7] This model is enormously powerful and seems to have the advantage of describing the creation of medieval studies as a progression from the darkness of pre-rational thought to the enlightenment of modern thinking. It narrates how the object of scholarly study was finally separated from the subject of the scholar, a separation which in turn seemed to promise an objective approach to premodernity.[8] As medievalism has gained legitimacy, increasing numbers of critics have made the case that amateur approaches to history might offer us access to different forms of time.[9] Yet even as these treatments laudably call for a dissolution of these binaries, they sometimes perpetuate the binaries that they mean to disassemble. For instance, Dinshaw separates the two by pointing to two different temporalities: regulated time that is 'abstract, objective, and countable'; and unregulated time that can start and stop at will. As Rick Godden has suggested (and as Dinshaw's meditations on her own 'amateurism' imply), for twenty-first-century academics and non-academics alike, these two kinds of time are almost always mixed up.[10] That they are sometimes seen as separate is a symptom not of their difference but of their similarity. The insistence on the distinction (which actually comes quite late) was generated by the anxiety that professional impulses were always wrapped up in the amatory, or amateur, aspects of medievalism.

But if these two groups have been and are historically linked, how to explain the animus between them? We argue that what governs the distrust (or impatience) of the amateur for the professional or the professional for the amateur is *how* one connects to the past.[11] The etymology for amateur (from the Latin, *amator* – lover) gestures to why non-professional connections to the Middle Ages are often characterised as amatory. This abstract and perhaps even spiritual connection seems enthusiastically to overleap time.

Professional connections to the medieval, on the other hand, are often enabled by what might be called the go-between of extant manuscripts and material culture. There is a desire for the past here, but there is a deep suspicion about the ability of love to unite us with that past. These different kinds of connections were then seen to do different kinds of work – feeling and knowing were constructed as non-convergent precisely because the entire history of the discipline was implicated in the connection between the two modes.

Is love for the past the same as desire for the past?

Nowhere is this interpenetration of amateurism and professionalism more apparent than in one of the narratives that is often adduced to demonstrate the way medieval studies professionalised itself. According to this history, Thomas Tyrwhitt's 1775 edition of Chaucer marked the beginning of the separation between professional and 'dilettante'.[12] This 'proto-professionalism' enabled the movement from the relative disorder of Thomas Speght's early modern editions of Chaucer to something resembling the modern editions that are in use today.[13] Tyrwhitt's great learning, his editorial principles and, perhaps most famously, his denigration of earlier editors ('it would be a waste of time to sift accurately the heap of rubbish which was added, by John Stowe, to the Edit. of 1561')[14] have led critics to see his work as a break from that of earlier, less enlightened editors and publishers. And it is quite possible that he saw himself in this way. In fact, until Richard Morris's 1866 revision of the Aldine Chaucer, Tyrwhitt's edition was acknowledged as authoritative. Yet if Tyrwhitt seems the very model of a modern Chaucerian editor, his involvement in the publication of what were thought to be the poems of the fifteenth-century monk Thomas Rowley reveals his deep desire to connect to the past on something other than an objective scholarly basis.

Two years after the publication of *The Canterbury Tales*, Tyrwhitt edited a collection of poetry entitled *Poems, supposed to have been written at Bristol, by Thomas Rowley, and others, in the fifteenth century*. Tyrwhitt is usually credited with the demonstration that these poems were forgeries by Thomas Chatterton; a claim that is in harmony with his customary position as first 'modern' Chaucerian editor.[15] And this claim, as far as it goes, is correct. But it was not in the first edition that he made this revelation, but rather in the appendix to the third edition in 1778. In the first edition, published anonymously (though it seems everyone knew Tyrwhitt was the editor) he does not expose these poems as forgeries; rather he is careful to express no firm opinion:

> It may be expected perhaps, that the Editor should give an opinion upon this important question; but he rather chooses, for many reasons, to leave it to the determination of the unprejudiced and intelligent Reader. He had long been desirous that these Poems should be printed; and therefore readily undertook the charge of superintending the edition. This he has executed in the manner, which seemed to him best suited to such a publication; and here he means that his task should end. Whether the Poems be really antient, or modern; the compositions of Rowley, or the forgeries of Chatterton; they must always be considered as a most singular literary curiosity.[16]

The circumspect nature of Tyrwhitt's preface appears to be an act of good faith. Luminaries such as Samuel Johnson thought the poems forgeries. Others thought them genuine medieval relics. Why not leave the determination of whether or not they were medieval to intelligent, objective readers? While this doesn't quite fly in the face of Tyrwhitt's methodologies as laid out in his edition of Chaucer (identifying what is genuinely by the poet, and what is not), it is telling that he suddenly resorts to crowd-sourcing issues of genuineness where elsewhere he insists that the true arbiter of genuineness would be one who has access to the manuscripts.[17] So why is he so equivocal here?

The answer is partly about desire. Tyrwhitt wished to hold on to the notion that the poems were genuine survivals. It is now known that Tyrwhitt was something of a Rowley enthusiast while he was working on his Chaucer edition.[18] In volume 3 he uses passages from 'Rowley's' works to explain a Chaucerian word and in volume 4 pleads for the publication of Rowley's poems. Even after Johnson and Thomas Warton express their belief that Rowley's works are actually written by Chatterton, Tyrwhitt maintains his belief in their genuineness and pursues his plans to publish.[19] But his reluctance to sound more decisive might also be explained by editorial scepticism: he had not seen the manuscripts in which the poems were supposedly found before the edition went to press. Only four months after he had submitted the edition did he travel to Bristol (apparently at the urging of Johnson) to see for himself the supposed manuscripts that were in the possession of the antiquarian surgeon William Barrett. Yet even these doubts did not prevent him from publishing. His rationale was to claim, surprisingly, that the poems' ancientness or modernity was really irrelevant to whether or not they should be printed because they had value as 'literary curiosities'.

Tyrwhitt seems somewhat caught out here. He makes the claim that, whether medieval or medievalist, the poems should have equal claim to our attention and it doesn't matter if we can't tell the difference. It is possible, of course, that we should take Tyrwhitt at his word. The forgeries of Chatterton had certainly become famous by the time of Tyrwhitt's third edition if not before, and Tyrwhitt's editions were quite successful. Considering his failure to consult the 'manuscripts' of Rowley's poems before he went to press, however, it is likely that Tyrwhitt's enthusiasm and his desire to believe that Rowley's poems were genuinely medieval got the better of him.

This enthusiasm is all the more remarkable given that not only Johnson and Warton, but even the exemplary dilettante and practitioner of medievalism Horace Walpole had long believed 'Rowley's' poems to be forgeries by Chatterton. Unfortunately for him, this fact led to a story that his refusal to publish the works of 'Rowley' in 1769 had led to Chatterton's suicide.[20] As a result, a large section of the public unjustly blamed Walpole for Chatterton's death. And so it was cold comfort when Walpole was finally able to write in 1778, 'If Mr. Tyrwhitt has opened his eyes to Chatterton's forgeries, there is an instance of conviction against strong prejudice! I have drawn up an account of my transaction with that marvellous young man [Chatterton], but I do not intend to print it.'[21] Like many received narratives that claim to delineate the move from amateur to professional, this one is from the outset far less schematic than it first appears. One who has been reckoned something of a medievalist dilettante uses his powers of reason to uncover the spuriousness of a faked past.[22] Our exemplar of proto-professional critical behaviour indulges his desire to declare this faked past authentic, or at least possibly authentic without adhering to the methodology that he himself laid out. Or perhaps it does not even matter. Once confronted with evidence of fraud, he has a change of heart, declares the fake past that he authenticated inauthentic and then receives credit for doing so. Meanwhile, our dilettante is haunted for the next twenty years with the slander that his rejection of the fake past led to the death of the youth whom William Wordsworth called the 'marvellous boy'. At the very outset of an influential narrative about the establishment of professionalism, our proto-professional is implicated in a medievalist passion for pastiche that he maintains in the face of overwhelming evidence that his passion is misplaced.

If we wished to rescue this narrative, we could say our hero Tyrwhitt fell temporarily into an antiquarian way of thinking (or rather, feeling) that betrayed him precisely because it was amateurish, more a reflection of the seeker than the sought. His penance then would be to renounce this desire (as he did) and return to methods of editing that foreground a rational, professional approach. The story could then be a cautionary tale outlining the dangers of becoming too close to the object of one's study. Such an approach could redraw the lines of professional and amateur and appeal to those who shudder at the prospect of amateurish error (something we have talked about above). But what of the strange passion for the lost Chatterton? Is it possible to dismiss it as a bit of romantic nostalgia for lost youth? Something more seems at work here – a kind of emotional connection that holds out a greater promise for the love associated with medievalism.

If we return to the 'amateur' Walpole, we find an example of such love. At first blush this love seems to exemplify precisely what we might expect: Walpole's investment in contemporary medievalism to the exclusion of the truly medieval. Just four years after the appearance of Tyrwhitt's edition of Rowley, Walpole famously wrote to his friend William Mason, in order to turn down his offer of 'a Blackletter Chaucer of the first edition' for a guinea, writing 'I am too, though a Goth, so modern a Goth that I hate the Black letter and I love Chaucer better in Dryden and Baskerville than in his own language and dress'.[23] Walpole's comment is generally seen as proof of the general obscurity of Chaucer in the eighteenth century, or Walpole's own unfamiliarity with Chaucer's text, or of the desire of Walpole and other 'Gothicists' to 'fabricate a pseudo-medievalism for modern tastes' rather than study 'authentic Middle English writings'.[24] What has generally been ignored is Walpole's own expression of love for Chaucer. And indeed, it might simply be a kind of throwaway line – 'love' here standing in for 'appreciate' or 'prefer'. Yet there may be more going on in this apparent rejection of the Blackletter Chaucer than first meets the eye.

Quotations of Walpole's letter almost always omit the second half of his comment: 'still my antiquarianility is much obliged to your pimping for it'.[25] Walpole's jocular transformation of the exchange with Mason into a transaction codes the Blackletter as a form of prostitute, but not one in which he is interested because he cannot abide its 'old' language and dress. Like the Wife of Bath, he prefers something a bit younger, the Baskerville font, for instance, which was only twenty-four years old. In this case, the clothes really do make the man, as the love expressed is for Chaucer in the latest attire. Yet strangely this is not a straightforward homosocial love for another man – instead Walpole allegorises desire as his own 'antiquarianility' (a word coined by Mason). Walpole's medievalism is especially complicated because it is not merely coded as the modern love for that which is old and the desire to recreate it (as he had at Strawberry Hill), but the desire for an updated 'oldness' that is easily accessible. And his desire for a medievalist 'new' Chaucer is not a desire for a medievalised as opposed to a medieval Chaucer. Rather it is a choice between medievalisms. Because, of course, what Walpole hates here is not really 'Chaucer in his own dress' at all – what he purports to hate is the sixteenth-century Blackletter that pretends to the way that Chaucer originally appeared in manuscript.

It is worth remembering here that this is the same man who sixteen years earlier had claimed the *Castle of Otranto* was not written by him, but 'was found in the library of an ancient Catholic family in the north of England' and 'was printed at Naples, *in the black letter*, in the year 1529' (our emphasis). His hatred, then, is not for Blackletter itself, but for the appearance of an authentic medieval text in the dress that mimics the manuscript. A fake manuscript may well lay claim to a kind of antiquity without cheapening itself because there is no authenticity to cheapen. But an authentic old text should not 'mimic' its own antiquity; it should be freshened up to be attractive. The antiquarianility, then, becomes a desire that is satisfied not by oldness seeming old, but by oldness recreated young – a medievalism that in its recreation of the old actually satisfies antiquarian desire. Walpole's love for Chaucer seems based on some essential trait that goes beyond the way the text appears on the page, or even (since he prefers Dryden's translation) beyond the text itself. And unlike the wholesale invention of the medievalist fictions in which he himself indulged, this medievalism or antiquarianility would not only retain its connection to the Middle Ages but would enable a greater amatory attachment to the medieval poet. The basis for this attachment, then, is not the book or the manuscript but a more abstract sense of the work; that is, as Maurice Blanchot puts it, 'hidden, radically absent perhaps, covered up in any case, obfuscated by the visibility of the book'.[26] Walpole's love did not so much embrace a faux version of the author as abstract a notion of the author himself that was available for amatory attachment. In this way the antiquarians maintained a connection with their objects of study even as they implied that the material object itself was only some poor shadow of the ideal, or one might say, platonic version of the work.

To know him is to love him

Yet if this platonic love was what motivated antiquarians in the eighteenth century, it was reoriented to return to a kind of materialist project in the nineteenth. The principal example of this reoriented love was F. J. Furnivall, who perversely based his love for Chaucer on the ways printed editions interfered with the possibility of cathexis with the medieval poet. His manifesto for the Chaucer Society explicitly outlined how it was 'to do honour to Chaucer, and to let lovers and students of him see how far the best unprinted manuscripts of his works differ from the printed texts'.[27] Later he would write, 'any one who reads the Canterbury Tales, and gets to know the man Chaucer, must delight in and love him' and later still in explaining the goals of the Society, he confesses his 'love for Chaucer' who comes 'closer to me than any other poet except Tennyson'.[28] The use of the spatial metaphor certainly expresses a kind of metaphoric affective closeness, but it also suggests how distance, whether metaphoric or literal, whether in terms of geography or time, can be defeated by love whose whole purpose is to make the lover and the beloved close.

To know Chaucer is to love him. And to love him is to see how he was represented in the manuscripts that were closest to him. Enthusiasm here is a direct result of the ability to know the object of contemplation. Unlike Walpole, whose love is based on some extra-philological essence of the poet that can be recuperated best through modernisations, Furnivall's love is the product of philological recovery. He thus stands somewhere between being a critical medievalist and one who 'betrays' the affect of the enthusiast. As Donald Baker writes, 'it will not do to leave the impression of Furnivall as *merely* an inspired textual amateur' (our emphasis).[29] He seems, in other words, to offer a kind of bridge between the medievalist love of the antiquarian and the critical rationality of the medievalist.[30]

But if nineteenth-century professions of love were calculated to aid the critical study of the medieval, their shelf life turned out to be remarkably short. It took less than a quarter of a century for a cool professionalism to displace Furnivallian enthusiasm. As Derek Brewer puts it:

> the year 1933 seemed to mark the decisive point of change in the balance between the amateur and professional criticism of Chaucer. It marked the point of overlap between the long tradition of the amateur critic – amateur both as lover and as unprofessional – and the beginning of the professional, even scientific criticism in which the concept of love of an author would too often appear ridiculous.[31]

The publication of F. N. Robinson's complete works of Chaucer (1933) *seemed* to crystallise and highlight a distinction between the amateur and professional reader of Chaucer. In fact the great virtue of Robinson's edition was seen to be its acknowledgement of the separation between 'the general reader ... and the proficient scholar' and its ability to appeal to 'the teacher *and* the amateur of Chaucer' (our emphasis).[32] As one of us has claimed elsewhere in slightly different terms, if Furnivall professed his closeness to Chaucer, 'modern scholars [were] careful to define a greater distance between themselves and Furnivall'.[33]

However, if institutional professions of love became unfashionable in the increasingly professionalised ranks of the university, this did not mean that love was abandoned in discussions of medieval texts. In fact, as medievalists well know, the exegetical mode of reading, as it became known, depended on Augustine's injunction that the text 'should be subjected to diligent scrutiny until an interpretation contributing to the reign of *caritas* is produced'.[34] In its apparent historicism, exegetics seemed to offer a counterbalance to what some viewed as the solipsism of New Critical methods. And in its Pauline elevation of *caritas* to the pinnacle of the interpretive process it seemed to ground the meanings of texts in the most important book of the medieval period rather than the psychological states of modern readers. It seemed, in a word, stable: not an embarrassing invocation of affect but a historically based hermeneutical principle that could govern the interpretation and recuperation of texts. Better yet, it required the study of paleography, languages and codicology and so offered medieval studies a way to legitimate its own existence as a form of *scientia*.

The subordination of interpretation to *caritas* has been widely criticised as assuming the reading that is to be produced before one even approaches the text to be interpreted. The totalising effects of such a circular hermeneutic have been laid out most trenchantly by Lee Patterson: 'the text produced by such an exegesis perfectly replicates the form of medieval culture as a whole, for it subordinates a wide range of disparate and potentially conflicting elements to the authority of an abstract *sententia*. And ... that *sententia* is always and everywhere the same.'[35] The understanding of the Middle Ages produced by such an approach necessarily sees the period as a univocal whole.

Even more damning was the suspicion that such a cool, historical approach completely submerged any humanity that one might find in the text by evacuating the love from love. If, as D. W. Robertson claimed, 'the function of the medieval poet was not so much to express his personal moods or emotions', many critics feared that such an approach might completely suppress the ability of literature to elicit emotion.[36] One of the most important expressions of this demurral can be found in Jill Mann's well-known essay on Troilus's swoon:

> there is no need to attack or defend the love-affair, and particularly Troilus' role in it, in historical terms. We not only can, but need to, respond directly to the emotions and instincts involved. If this discussion, then, has any implications for new directions in Chaucer studies, they are that we should, in a sense, go back to the old directions, and abandon some of our self-conscious historicism in order to examine Chaucer's representations of human relationships with no other preconceptions than our belief that a poet of profound humanity will have something complex and enriching to show us in them.[37]

Patterson argues that Mann's 'apparently superfluous dismissal' of 'self-conscious historicism' demonstrates 'a powerfully felt' but 'unarticulated' antagonism 'to the explicitly historicist claims of Exegetics'.[38] In the sense that Mann does not articulate an argument in strictly intellectual terms, Patterson may be correct, but, of course, part of her point is precisely that an overintellectualised historicism will sunder us from Chaucer's meaning. Mann further claims that any articulation of what literature is supposed to do can be found 'not [in] literary conventions or religious doctrine or social orthodoxy', but 'in the special "binding" of love' that is itself based 'on the "lawe of kynde" which Chaucer must have trusted would work as powerfully on his twentieth-century readers as on his fourteenth-century ones'.[39]

Late modern critics might well distrust such an open naturalisation of affect, and specifically love, as the basis for the reception of medieval literature. But the power of this affective assault on exegetics was decisive. And with the advent of the crisis of the humanities, some would return to affect as the singular mark of literature – a move that can be encapsulated in Simon During's plea for a neo-amatory literary criticism:

> What is finally at stake in any attempt to move beyond what is increasingly looking like the stalled and demoralized field of literary studies is a recovery of what has been lost in the three positions I have outlined: that is, a commitment to a particular form of Subjectivity – literary subjectivity – characterized by a love of literature ...[40]

For During, the literary subjectivity that can be recuperated through the love of literature offers a way to reinvigorate a field under attack from within the university and without. The study of literature had lost what made it distinctive, the ability to (in the words of J. Hillis Miller) be carried away into a ' "virtual reality" ... to enter that imaginary space only by yielding to the magic incantation of the words on the page'.[41] The amatory here is translated into 'magic' by Miller – a move that During also makes by returning to an older idea of literature, citing the 'magic hand' of art in Thomas Warton's sonnet 'Written after seeing Wilton-House'.

As one of the more important advocates of affect, Nicholas Watson made the case for a hermeneutics of empathy in his reading of reactions to Carolyn Walker Bynum's *Holy Feast and Holy Fast* – arguing that we should treat the Middle Ages less like an other and more, in some sense, like a beloved.[42] So too, Aranye Fradenburg, following up on her earlier critique of a hermeneutics of suspicion, calls for a contemporary medieval studies to 'become medieval': not to identify with the past, but to allow our enthusiasm for it to 'exchange actions and passions with it or to join with it in composing a more powerful body'.[43] And David Wallace, while acknowledging that any recuperation of the medieval requires us to take account of 'the conditions of its transmission', suggests that 'it is perhaps time to emphasize (to hear again) the phenomenality of voice'.[44] In all three instances, we hear a desire to restore what seems to have become lost as medievalists have assiduously hedged in and bracketed off the Middle Ages as unattainable.

Of course, this appreciation for a rhetoric of affect is part of a much larger critical interest in the history and ethics of emotions. But it is possible that the case for a specifically medieval affect is a special one. Both Watson and Fradenburg, for instance, invoke the mystical love of medieval women (though to somewhat different effect) in order to suggest that this kind of love might model an approach to the past.[45] They assert that such empathetic feelings might make permeable the boundary between subject and object. As one medieval mystic (quoted by Fradenburg) puts it, 'Qwhat is lufe bott transfourmynge of desire / In to þe þinge lufyd'.[46] Particularly in the case of Watson, the medieval contemplative desire for God provides a framework for the modern scholar's desire for the past.[47] This is the hope of a love more than human that underpins the ability to recuperate the past.

At its best, the effect of these feelings is magical. Though Wallace does not delve as deeply into the rationale for an affective approach to the past, he nonetheless claims, 'there is, I think, something magical in the business of bringing back texts, voices from forgotten places, into the present'.[48] Fradenburg describes this magic as necromantic as she analogises 'intelligible things that channelled magical power from the dead to the living' with medieval texts.[49] And Watson asserts that far from criticising medievalists like Caroline Walker Bynum for being 'shamanistic', we should embrace her methodology as 'magical', both because it is desirable to hear the voices of the past in this form of 'storytelling', and also because it is naive to believe that we can ever escape 'ghostly ways of speaking'.[50] Watson's latter claim, a reversal of the hermeneutics of despair, is crucial for us because it suggests the possibility of what James Simpson has somewhat wryly characterised as 'an apostolic succession of continuous time'.[51]

As might be apparent from his comment, Simpson is not completely in sympathy with this enthusiastic accessibility of the past. In fact, he avers that 'by loving the object of our study as ourselves, we remain unknown to ourselves, precisely because we never know anything but our ever-absorptive, ever self-confirming selves'.[52] Simpson's comment rehearses, to some extent, D. Vance Smith's claim (made at almost the same time) that the turn to affect, at least in the way Watson carries it out, 'is at heart a narcissistic project, and one founded on the European post-Enlightenment project of the elaboration of a pedagogy of sentiment'.[53] While Smith claims that such a project is anti-intellectual, Simpson goes further and suggests that such enthusiasm, particularly at a time of growing religious fundamentalism, is positively dangerous.

Both critiques are powerful and we take it as an indication of the scale of such objections that Watson has very publicly recanted, saying 'the focus of "Desire for the Past" on scholarly affect has come to seem too personal to have much bearing on the larger challenge posed to our relationship with the past by modernity'.[54] In Watson's rethinking of his position we are struck by the extent to which he represents personal feeling and response as too insignificant upon which to base a theory of one's relationship to the Middle Ages. All literary criticism and scholarship is, of course, in some sense personal. But what we understand him to mean by personal is ultimately too involved with the dyadic pairing of lover and beloved, and hence not accessible by others outside this relationship. In a sense, Watson's hesitation about his own claims suggests that the results of his 'experiment' are not repeatable because the experience of empathy or love is far too varied among different individuals to be of use to the larger field. Smith and Simpson's objection is a bit different. They believe one might well run the experiment and, in a particular time period, and a particular place, have a large number of people agree, but that this agreement tells us a lot less about the past and a lot more about the make-up and identity of this particular group.

We will have more to say about the epistemological legitimacy of these hesitations below, but for now it is important to understand the practical implications of an abandonment of affect as a recuperative method. We hope our short history of love demonstrates that the appeal of, and justification for, the study of the Middle Ages has always had an affective basis. And though there may be times when we are too enamoured of a particular reading or attribution, we maintain that simply to ignore or suppress love, passion or desire as amateurish is to fall back into an impoverished vocabulary that threatens to doom our 'profession'. We want to be very careful here. If we cannot express our own desire to love the Middle Ages, if we cannot be unembarrassed by a desire to get closer to the medieval, then why would anyone else understand the nature of our commitment? This might seem to confuse the justification for the study of the Middle Ages with the ability to recuperate the past, but it seems to us that to divorce our desire for the Middle Ages from the means by which we can get closer to it is to make our commitment to the Middle Ages unintelligible. This problem has not escaped the critics of empathic understanding. Perhaps no one is clearer about this than Simpson, who says 'for the scholar in the museum, scholarship is mortuary work, prompted by tears at the fragmented tomb, while the scholar of continuous temporality enjoys an erotics of study'.[55] The issue, then, seems not to be whether affect will affect the recuperation of the Middle Ages, or the history of medieval emotions and feelings, but what kind of affect medievalists wish to indulge and embrace. Does one wish to be the melancholic scholar who is continually afraid of losing the past and attempts to hold on to it even as she or he knows it is lost? Or can love make the dead truly live?

But perhaps these choices represent a false dilemma. The choice between the melancholia of a John Leland or the rapturous love of a Julian may mask something at work here.[56] In other words, this choice obscures the very instrumentality that complicates the recovery of the past; there is nearly always a third term that mediates the relationship between the present and the past. This third term is evident in Wallace's call for more attention to the circumstances underwriting the transmission of medieval texts. Specifically, his assertion that the 'urnlike integrity' of medieval texts should be challenged because transmission so often alters the received text gestures to a study not of the lover and the beloved, or the mourner and mourned, but of what can only be called, in the erotics of literary recuperation, the 'go between' or in the resuscitation of the past, the 'medium'.[57] We would suggest, then (using Wallace's iteration of the phenomenality of voice), that there are other 'alien' voices that at once enable and threaten our relationship with the past. We turn to these embodied and disembodied voices in the hope that they can clarify our relationship to the past as well as the relationship of medievalism to the medieval.

Alien voices

Watson's initial claim – that we should desire a kind of channelled version of the Middle Ages – seems contentious not so much because it is narcissistic, but because of the different kinds of voices that one encounters in this shamanistic recovery. This uncertainty about whom, precisely, we might be addressing when we 'channel' the Middle Ages is apparent to Watson, for in adapting Dinshaw's haptic notion of a relationship to the Middle Ages, he downplays the risks of shamanism by translating the shamanistic metaphor 'into terms more familiar to medievalists'.[58] Specifically, he would like us to think more in terms of the mystic's than the shaman's voice. Such a translation, of course, is not objectionable on the face of it, but it does eliminate certain problems that remain if we continue to think of Walker Bynum's magical 'storytelling' in shamanistic terms. Shamans had access both to good and evil spirits while mystics claimed, at least, that the source of their voice was God.

If certain mystics were distrusted by their audiences (and one certainly thinks of Margery here), they nonetheless claimed that their visions originated with, or at least were permitted by, the divine. Watson qualifies this affinity between medieval scholarship and mystic vision in his later essay on imagination in speaking about 'the risk of error', but he also explains how the risk-taking seemed justified both because the rewards were so great and because the risk seemed small.[59] No such stricture exists when one is speaking of shamans – for the magic that they offer is very different from the miraculous 'magic' of Christian mysticism.

In other words, Watson invokes Christian mysticism as a particular model of magical communication that already contains within it the probability that the person one is speaking to is the person to whom one wishes to speak. To be fair, Watson seems a bit discomfited by the full force of his mystical metaphor. He urges his readers to contribute hermeneutic suspicion where it is lacking and reminds us that it is impossible to have a completely empathetic connection with a past that is so fragmented.[60] Yet in a quotation from the fourteenth-century mystic Richard Rolle, Watson demonstrates how complete the empathetic connection between God and his worshipper should be. Rolle exhorts a woman reader to love God and 'gyf hym halely thi hert' and warns her that 'Iwhils thi hert is heldande to luf of any bodyly thyng, thou may not parfitly be cupilde wit God'.[61] The language of mysticism, as is so apparent here, is not about partial connections with the divine, nor imperfect devotion, but surrender. And indeed, Watson is forced to distance himself from the quotation almost as he quotes it, saying, 'there is in any case no possibility of being "parfitly cupilde" with anything in the past; all we ever have is fragments'.[62] This is not to suggest that Watson's insight (or for that matter Fradenburg's or Wallace's) about the magical qualities of hearing voices from the past is to be dismissed; rather it is to understand that the voices we hear won't necessarily be saying just one thing. As Larry Scanlon has pointed out, 'the basic question for the historian is "what happened?" For a literary scholar, the basic question is "what is a particular text trying to say?"'[63] We would go further and say that whether one is a literary critic or historian, to attend to the voice or voices of a text, one needs to engage affectively with a text, and the way those voices are heard. Whatever *we* think of affect as a medium for the recovery of the past, medieval men and women certainly believed that it gave *them* access to the past. If we are to argue against affect, then, one of our strategies must be to say that just because we as medievalists study medieval men and women, we do not need to try to become like them. We do not have to (in fact it may be impossible) 'get medieval'. As has perhaps become evident, we do not seek to draw hard and fast battle lines between those who wish to take affect seriously as a mode of recovery and those who do not. Rather, we are attempting to show the different ways the desire to know the past can become the desire to inhabit the past: in a weak sense, this is the distinction between medieval studies and medievalism.

Without giving too much weight to this distinction, it nevertheless helps to clarify the stakes for this argument and also enables us to rethink two important terms that define the debate between medieval studies and medievalism: history and memory. As one might well expect, almost all of the interlocutors in the debate tend to speak in terms of history. Smith notes, 'Dinshaw's work so far has been to permit the citation of affectivity as the rubric under which otherwise conventional history proceeds'.[64] Simpson makes the case for a *muséal* understanding when he writes 'given the true and deep continuities of our history, we cannot simply convert back to a pre-museum culture'.[65] Watson, meanwhile, writes of the 'redemption of history' in his earlier article and the promise of 'our own activities as historians' in his later essay.[66] These invocations of history seem completely appropriate, as history would appear to be the rubric under which critical medieval studies unites its multitude of different disciplines.

Yet it might be worthwhile also to use the extensive work in memory studies to buttress our relationship to the past. Watson carries out a bit of this work, focusing on the imaginative recombination of that which is recollected from the collective *memoria* or archive.[67] But these memories always tend to appear beneath the sign of 'theories of history'.[68] Given Watson's ambitions to provide a less personal (more communal) theory of the past, this makes perfect sense. And we do not advocate a position that absolutely opposes history to memory. But it is well to remember that when the mystics write of their abilities to 'see' the past they invariably speak in memorial terms. Julian of Norwich describes how in the eighth shewing her 'body was fulfillid of feling and mynd [memory] of Crists passion and His deth'.[69] She explains that 'whan we have minde of his blessed passion with pitte and love, then we suffer with him, like as his frendes did that saw it'.[70] Medievalists have long understood this kind of ritualistic memory to be at the heart of the commemorative processes that enable an understanding of time as cyclic and liturgical as opposed to linear and secular. As Gabrielle Spiegel has suggested, linear time, or what is often thought as history, can be ritualised through memory. The passion of Christ thus exists in the here and now for mystics like Julian. And even within the liturgy and perhaps even some drama, 'mimetic action may be an important part' but 'its main purpose is rather to effect a change from spectator to participant, from the feeling of "like" to "is"'.[71] But for Spiegel, 'to the extent that memory "resurrects", "recycles", and makes the past "reappear" and live again in the present, it cannot perform historically, since it refuses to keep the past in the past'.[72] The job of history is to 're-present'; the job of memory is 're-member' in order to 're-vivify' the corpse. One faces towards the past, the other faces towards the future. One, as a number of critics have suggested, is analytic or critical and the other is affective.

Such claims about the differentiation of memory and history are tempting and enable us to make large claims about how modern critical practice is differentiated from antique memorial practice, but as Paul Strohm has suggested, such claims are ultimately unsustainable because 'the seal between past and present ... never really existed'.[73] As he says, quoting Augustine's famous meditation on time, 'we have only the present ... a "present of the past" ("praesens de praeteritis") and a "present of the future" ("praesens de futuris"), with both past and future eternally present as memory and expectation'.[74] The great illusion here (as Augustine knew well) is that memory is simply present as opposed to a thing that is the product of the action, sometimes even the labour of remembering. Memory in this formulation is both the medium that recovers the past and the image of the past. While we make a natural separation between the thing I have remembered and the remembered thing, in the absence of some reason for disbelief, we assume that the two are relatively close. In modern terms, this belief is based on the idea that the rememberer has experienced the event or thing to be remembered. Pierre Nora and others have made larger claims about the existence of collective memory, although these claims have come under considerable attack.[75] To make claims about remembering when one has not personally experienced the thing to be remembered confuses lived memories with transmitted history.[76] But, as Marianne Hirsch has argued, there is a contemporary mode of mind that is similitudinous to the feeling of memory. It 'is not identical to memory: it is "post", but at the same time, it approximates memory in its affective force'.[77]

Medieval thinkers had no need to construct what Hirsch calls 'postmemory' because implicit within the idea of memory was the notion that something could be called memory even as it was not 'lived' in the modern sense. Crucially, there was also a sense that it was analogous to rather than identical with the memory that was felt. As Julian suggests in her recollection of the Passion, when we remember, we suffer with Christ '*like* as his frendes did that saw it'. Memory here can be close enough that it fills the body with feeling, maybe even the feeling that we are witnessing *the* Passion, but it does not make us identical with those who witnessed it. Memory here is a medium that seems to be metaphorical. It appears to transport us literally to another time, but it is in fact analogical. It might appear that in seeming 'real' this form of memory is false. But this would be to conflate issues of identity with truth claims about what one has remembered and it is to think of memory only in mimetic terms.

In a sense what we are arguing is not so different from what David Freedberg, Alfred Gell and, most recently, C. Stephen Jaeger have argued – that texts (perhaps agentially) work to elicit certain reactions from their audiences.[78] We would also claim that the way these texts elicit a reaction is by activating memory, leading us (in that now hoary, hyphenated phrase) to re-member what one could not possibly have witnessed. Is there one particular way in which one needs to remember? In other words, does each text have one reconstruction that is 'right'? Or at least more right than others? This is a question of interpretation that depends both on the ability to recreate a text and the ability to recreate the feelings that the text calls forth. Such a critical sense, for want of a better word, will not proceed from a merely rational and objective weighing of historical evidence. Nor will it emerge from a totalising theoretical structure even if, like exegetics, that structure seems to ground itself in history. Instead the reader has to grant the text a kind of subjective presence. Some will say that they have this presence because we grant it to them, that reading texts this way is to impose a 'nonmedieval' aesthetic sense on them. We argue that it is more complicated than this, that to come to texts with ready-made assumptions about what is medieval and what is not is to resist the subjectivity of the text. Such a process is risky. Our passion for the past could lead to errors – even ones that might seem, to some, amateurish. But it seems preferable to risk error than to embrace a cautious professionalism that codes the Middle Ages as distant, remote and all but unreachable.

Notes

1. Barnes, *The Sense of an Ending*, p. 3.
2. Prendergast and Trigg, 'What is happening to the Middle Ages?'.
3. Prendergast and Trigg, 'What is happening to the Middle Ages?'.
4. For an early and engaging example, see Lindley, 'The ahistoricism of medieval film'.
5. Eco, 'Dreaming of the Middle Ages', p. 68.
6. Eco, 'Dreaming of the Middle Ages', pp. 70–1.
7. See, for instance, Matthews, 'What was medievalism?', pp. 9–22.
8. See Utz, *Chaucer and the Discourse of German Philology*, pp. 116–17.
9. Elements of this critique can be found (in different ways) in the works of David Matthews and Richard Utz. But the most sustained case for the amateur versus the professional is Carolyn Dinshaw's *How Soon Is Now?*
10. Godden, 'Nerds, love, amateurs'.
11. Dinshaw, *How Soon Is Now?*, p. 26.
12. Ruggiers (ed.), *Editing Chaucer*, p. 6.
13. Dinshaw, *How Soon Is Now?*, p. 26. Matthews, 'What was medievalism?'.
14. Tyrwhitt (ed.), *The Canterbury Tales*, p. xxii.
15. Windeatt, 'Thomas Tyrwhitt', p. 118. Forni, *The Chaucerian Apocrypha*, p. 145.
16. *Poems*, ed. Tyrwhitt, p. xii.
17. Windeatt, 'Thomas Tyrwhitt', p. 118.
18. Tyrwhitt (ed.), *The Canterbury Tales*, vol. 4, p. 87; vol. 3, p. 318.
19. Powell, 'Thomas Tyrwhitt', pp. 314–26.
20. The attack on Walpole was apparently a direct result of the publication of Tyrwhitt's edition in February of 1777.
21. Cunningham (ed.), *The Letters of Horace Walpole*, vol. 7, p. 77. Ultimately he printed two hundred copies and gave them away.
22. Walpole's letter to Chatterton is lost, but Chatterton prepared a reply (which he failed to send) suggesting that Walpole (and his friends) felt the metre too modern. See Lewis (ed.), *The Yale Edition of Horace Walpole's Correspondence*, vol. 16, p. 112.
23. Mitford (ed.), *The Correspondence of Horace Walpole*, vol. 2, pp. 203, 205.
24. Miskimin, 'The illustrated eighteenth-century Chaucer', p. 32; Sabor, 'Medieval revival and the gothic', pp. 474–5.
25. Mitford (ed.), *The Correspondence of Horace Walpole*, vol. 2, p. 203. Part of the reason for this omission may be that the phrase is seen as referring to a portrait of Drayton, but the adversative clearly refers back to the Chaucer.
26. Qtd in Smith, 'The inhumane wonder of the book', p. 361.
27. Qtd in Munro (ed.), *Frederick James Furnivall*, p. xlix.
28. Furnivall, *A Temporary Preface*, pp. 2–3.
29. Baker, 'Frederick James Furnivall', p. 166.
30. We have both written on Furnivall's enthusiasm: Prendergast, *Chaucer's Dead Body*, passim; but see, especially, Trigg, *Congenial*

Souls, pp. 160–73. And for a reading of Furnivall's enthusiasm as embarrassing, see Santini, *The Impetus of Amateur Scholarship*, p. 192. Dinshaw maintains her focus on the difference between amateur and professional temporalities when discussing Furnivall, but acknowledges the complexity of attaching the label of 'amateur' to one who played such an important role in the genealogy of the '*profession* of medievalist' (*How Soon Is Now?*, p. 26).

31 Brewer, *Chaucer: The Critical Heritage*, vol. 2, p. 1.
32 Utz quotes from reviews of Robinson by J. S. P. Tatlock and Martin B. Rudd ('The colony writes back', n. 51). Even if the transition from Furnivall to Robinson was seen as a progression from amateurism to professionalism, Utz has argued that the unacknowledged history of later nineteenth- and early twentieth-century Chaucer criticism was considerably more complex – involving national and epistemological agendas. And Robinson's own edition was notable not in its break with the past as for its reliance on earlier print editions.
33 Trigg, *Congenial Souls*, p. 183.
34 Augustine, *On Christian Doctrine*, p. 93. Robertson avoids the moral neutrality of the word *amor* by focusing on the Augustinian split between *caritas* 'the love of God, self and neighbor only for God's sake' and *cupiditas* 'the love of anything at all without reference to God' (Newman, *God and Goddesses*, p. 141).
35 Patterson, *Negotiating the Past*, p. 32.
36 Robertson, Jr., *A Preface to Chaucer*, p. 15.
37 Mann, 'Troilus' swoon', p. 332.
38 Patterson, *Negotiating the Past*, p. 6.
39 Mann, 'Troilus' swoon', p. 332.
40 During, 'Literary subjectivity', p. 39.
41 Miller, *Literature as Conduct*, p. 94.
42 Watson, 'Desire for the past', pp. 59–97.
43 Fradenburg, *Sacrifice Your Love*, p. 78. She is quoting Deleuze and Guattari, *A Thousand Plateaus*, p. 257. For her early critique of the 'othering' of the Middle Ages, see '"Voice Memorial"', pp. 169–202.
44 Wallace, *Premodern Places*, p. 17, n. 11.
45 See also Dinshaw's discussion of Margery Kempe in which she suggests that mystical openness gives time a kind of agency: '"The Mystic is seized by time as by that which erupts and transforms", writes Michel de Certeau of the mystic's temporality, opposing it to the historian's chronological, classificatory handling of time' (*How Soon Is Now?*, p. 113).
46 This sentiment seems to be something of a guiding principle for Fradenburg, as she quotes Richard Misyn's translation of Richard Rolle's *Incendium Amoris* at least three times (*Sacrifice Your Love*, pp. 31, 73–4, 77).
47 Watson is, of course, careful to state that the analogy is not perfect ('Desire for the past', p. 97).

48 Wallace, *Premodern Places*, p. 9.
49 Fradenburg, *Sacrifice Your Love*, p. 58. However, she seems a bit more chary about the complete identification with the medieval that magic would signify. As she puts it, 'apotropaic identifications with the dead, and their management via techniques of living, are at work in both contemporary and medieval understandings of the ethics of historiography. Identification does not usually function now as it did then ... but the ambivalence of identification, mourning and melancholy are points of convergence between some of the signifying effects of medieval historical literature and (popular and academic) medievalism today' (*Sacrifice Your Love*, p. 56). Her hesitation certainly has to do with the violent erasure of difference in the other (the medieval) that such a complete identification would portend. But she also has a healthy respect for the medieval idea that magic, however 'wonderful', should be treated with suspicion as its source can either be angelic or demonic (*Sacrifice Your Love*, p. 272, n. 33).
50 Watson, 'Desire for the past', pp. 68, 69, 72.
51 Simpson, 'Not just a museum?', p. 141.
52 Simpson, 'Not just a museum?', p. 142.
53 Smith, 'The application of thought to medieval studies', p. 89.
54 Watson, 'The phantasmal past', pp. 3–4.
55 Simpson, 'Not just a museum?', p. 142.
56 Simpson's discussion of melancholia, Leland and English literary history can be found in *Reform and Cultural Revolution*, pp. 7–33.
57 Wallace (ed.), *The Cambridge History of Medieval English Literature*, p. xx.
58 Watson, 'Desire for the past', p. 68.
59 Watson, 'The phantasmal past', p. 25.
60 Watson, 'Desire for the past', pp. 84, 97.
61 The quotation is from Rolle's *Ego Dormio* and can be found in Horstman, *Yorkshire Writers*, pp. 1, 50. See Watson, 'Desire for the past', p. 96.
62 Watson, 'Desire for the past', p. 97.
63 Scanlon, 'Historicism: six theses'.
64 Smith, 'The application of thought to medieval studies', p. 86.
65 Simpson, 'Not just a museum?', p. 144.
66 Watson, 'Desire for the past', p. 62; Watson, 'The phantasmal past', p. 31.
67 Watson, 'The phantasmal past', p. 31.
68 Watson, 'The phantasmal past', p. 36.
69 *The Shewings of Julian of Norwich*, lines 2281–2.
70 Watson and Jenkins (eds), *The Writings of Julian of Norwich*, p. 365. The language of memory, of course, suffuses *The Book of Margery Kempe*. See Windeatt (ed.), *The Book of Margery Kempe*, pp. 186, 273,

275, 309. Thomas Bestul traces this form of reconstructive memory back at least as far as Anselm ('Antecedents', p. 6).
71 Vaughan, 'The three advents', p. 499.
72 Spiegel, 'Memory and historical time', p. 149.
73 Strohm, 'Rememorative reconstruction', p. 8.
74 Strohm, 'Rememorative reconstruction', p. 7.
75 Nora, 'Between memory and history', pp. 7–24. One of the more comprehensive attacks on Nora (and one quoted with approbation by Spiegel) and the idea of the 'memory industry' is Klein, 'On the emergence of *memory*', pp. 127–50.
76 Weissman, *Fantasies of Witnessing*, p. 17.
77 Hirsch, 'The generation of postmemory', p. 109.
78 Jaeger, *Enchantment*, p. 5.

5
Discontent in the age of mechanical reproduction

At the end of *Civilization and Its Discontents*, Freud famously recapitulates the thesis of his book by suggesting that something has altered the eternal struggle between Eros and Thanatos. Human aggression now has the capability to extinguish not just some lives, but all humankind and this, he claims, has led to 'their current unrest, their unhappiness and their mood of anxiety'.[1] It is futurity and the uncertainty of whether one will inhabit it that leads to the most profound discontent. We won't make such apocalyptic claims about the nature of medievalism and its discontents here, but it seems clear that medievalists have the capability to have a decisive impact on their own survival. So, to put it crudely: where do we go from here? We have suggested that our relations with the medieval past are often structured as affective histories. But just as importantly, we have tried to trace the genealogy of feelings about medievalism itself, which have not always been positive ones. What are the implications of all this discontent about medievalism for the future of medieval studies and medievalism? Are we all forever doomed to a future of mutual discontent with each other? Or can we unite in perpetual discontent with those outside both fields who, beyond the academy, continue to relegate the medieval to the most barbaric and irrelevant margins of modernity and, within it, to the most vulnerable extremes of a humanities syllabus in crisis? Is it possible to imagine a future of teaching and research in both fields that might operate according to a different dynamic? We would like to close our study by speculating about some possible futures for the medieval. We would also like to raise the stakes of the debate even higher. What can we learn about the way academic disciplines traditionally focus their greatest competitive energies – their discontent – onto the most adjacent fields? Is it possible to refocus those energies on to the more productive contributions medieval and medievalism studies might make to the future of the humanities, especially in the modern university?

As we have acknowledged, the relationship between the institutions of medieval studies and medievalism has become less stable and predictable than it was when we first conceived this project some years ago. We do not mean to measure and simply count the strength of numbers in the growth of the 'secondary' field, though the proliferation of sessions on medievalism at major conferences (Leeds, Kalamazoo, New Chaucer Society) is a clear indication of research interest in this area and the way medieval studies has opened up its gates to the newer critical field. The growth of university subjects, dissertations, published guides to, and studies of, medievalism also testify to greater interest in teaching and researching medievalism. We may also identify a renewed sophistication in much of the cultural and literary theory that informs many recent publications in medievalism studies. No longer is the dominant mode of medievalism studies simply the identification and description of medievalist elements in post-medieval culture, or arguments for the depth and breadth of medieval allusion. The most sophisticated and wide-ranging work in this field now participates in rich, diverse dialogues with other fields such as cinema studies, gender and race studies, historicism, colonialism, game theory, literary theory and fiction studies.[2]

Nor is the antagonism between medieval and medievalism studies as pronounced as it used to be. There are a number of recent studies, publications and working groups that have substantially and deliberately broken down many of the conventional distinctions between these fields. These range from archaeological and genealogical studies such as Bruce Holsinger's *The Premodern Condition*, Andrew Cole and Vance Smith's *The Legitimacy of the Middle Ages* and the revisionary queer historiographies of Carolyn Dinshaw's *Getting Medieval* and *How Soon Is Now?*; to political interventions that foreground the shaping role of medievalist thought (Holsinger's *Medievalism, Neo-Conservatism, and the War on Terror*); to revisionary literary histories such as James Simpson's *Reform and Cultural Revolution* and cultural histories such as John Ganim's *Medievalism and Orientalism*; to journals that actively signpost their commitment to a medievalist approach (e.g. *postmedieval*); and projects like 'Global Chaucers' that wind modern and global versions and translations of Chaucer into productive dialogue with Middle English texts. Social media also plays an important role in disseminating and promulgating a less formal version of medieval studies. On Twitter, in particular, scholars, students, novelists and enthusiasts of all kinds can share images, information and questions about the Middle Ages in a way that has the effect of breaking down some of the more formal academic hierarchies and disciplinary distinctions that have often set medieval and medievalism studies at odds with each other. And in a most conspicuous example, the HBO television series *Game of Thrones*, based on George R. R. Martin's *A Song of Ice and Fire*, regularly brings scholars and fans into the immediacy of online debate and discussion. Medievalism here generates a global community of historical scholarship, critical analysis and enthusiastic play.

In spite of these signs of rapprochement, however, one of our main starting-points or motivations for this book remains unresolved. The stand-off between medieval and medievalism studies does not appear so often in printed or oral discourse – partly because it would now sound so old-fashioned and defensive to complain about each other – but the shadow of that earlier mutual distrust still falls between the medieval and the medievalist. There still seems a stubborn suspicion in many quarters that medievalism offers a false object in place of a true medieval one while claiming that the false object is somehow constitutive of the true one; or, from the other point of view, that medieval studies is hopelessly invested in a backwards-looking positivistic project, denying academic positions and futures to (younger) scholars who might be able to revivify their discipline.

We have argued that the relationship between the medieval and the medievalist can no longer (if it ever could) be reduced to a simple hierarchy that could be seen as either chronologically or ontologically stable. Indeed, we think they are now irrevocably, and mutually (though unevenly) constitutive of each other. We also claim that a productive medievalist practice needs to take both fields into account. And yes, we deliberately use that adjective 'medievalist' to blur the familiar distinction. Not all the time, of course; it would be absurd to suggest that every article, chapter or lecture in the fields of medieval literature, medieval history and medievalism all need to reference materials and insights from those other fields. However, we think that to insist on a form of mutual exclusion, or the uncontaminated purity of one from the other, is not only intellectually misleading but also politically damaging. Both fields are under substantial threat in a Western university tradition that persistently and increasingly devalues non-vocational training: neither medieval studies nor medievalism studies can afford to slip into an old-style disciplinary regime that spends most of its energies policing its own borders against its nearest rivals. Instead, both fields have every reason to engage with contemporary debates about politics, meaning and culture; to articulate the power of literary and cultural texts, and patterns of historical change; to inform the way we track social change, the way our feelings of and knowledge about the past can change, and the relation between politics, society and the imagination.

We also advance the claim that medievalism – conceived most broadly as an engaged dialectic between the medieval past and the post-medieval future – is and/or could be seen as an exemplary discourse or practice in relation to the humanities and their understanding of history and culture. This practice would function not only in terms of the dominant thematic tropes of nostalgia or fascination with the abject; not even in terms of the emotional patterns of love and fear we have focused on, but in the very lure of the object, the artefact, the structuring narrative of the (scholarly) quest for truth, the lure of the aura of the past, the desire to find a past narrative or a mythic structure to serve as a mirror for ourselves, or to use as a springboard for revolutionary change.

The problem underlining all of these claims returns to the phenomena of loss and recovery. We have, a number of times in this book, made claims about the ability to recuperate the medieval via the medievalist that many may find naive, troubling or even flat out untrue. And we acknowledge that even the most rigorous 'historicist' project will necessarily come to a truth that is partial, fragmentary and ultimately unsatisfying. Medievalism and medieval studies both enact a form of Zeno's paradox. Little by little we break down the things that separate us from the past but in spite of all our scholarly labours and imaginative work, we will never ever get there in its full plenitude. This has led a number of those who study medievalism to embrace a relatively radical postmodern rejection of any idea of the original.

Specifically, the theoretical positionings of Jean Baudrillard have proved very influential on many who study medievalism. The powerful concept of the simulacrum seemed to capture the attenuated relationship of medievalism to medieval studies especially in what Baudrillard characterised as third order simulacra – 'no longer a question of imitation, nor duplication, nor even parody. It is a question of substituting the signs of the real for the real.'[3] As one critic put it, 'There is no longer any depth, any reality behind representation, only other representations'.[4] For Lauryn S. Mayer, the simulacrum structures a contrast between 'traditional medievalism', which is 'haunted' by its challenge to its desire to recreate the medieval past, and postmodernist or neomedievalism which deploys the simulacrum to critique those older forms.[5] This concept and way of thinking about 'copies' or 'simulations' was itself informed by the notion that while in the past a copy might actually have an original, postmodernity had moved on – '*never again* will the real have a chance to produce itself' (our emphasis).[6] The only thing that is left is nostalgia, for 'when the real is no longer what it was, nostalgia assumes its full meaning'.[7]

As is no doubt apparent, we have profound doubts about the radical scepticism underlying Baudrillard's theorising about the past. To say that any attempt to recuperate the past is simply a nostalgic attempt to recapture the lost and unattainable object of desire, or, in psychoanalytic terms, the *objet petit a*, seems reductive.[8] To say, as Baudrillard does, that 'today' (a word he uses obsessively) the copy has lost the ability to refer to the original seems itself a product of nostalgia generated less by any semiotic state of affairs than a theory of periodisation that relentlessly pursues a 'true present, a point of origin that marks a new departure'.[9] William Kuskin suggests that this is simply novelty's 'attempt to deny the past entirely in a bid for everlasting presence'.[10] To embrace such a theorisation of the present's connection to the past (or rather lack of connection) seems to us only another way of so completely othering the medieval that it can never speak.

A facsimile of the Middle Ages

To make our point we turn to a convergence of the medieval/medievalist phenomenon in order to recover what might be called the *quidditas* of the medieval. The example of the manuscript facsimile is a powerful and indicative one. These are objects used equally in research and in teaching, in the fields of art history, textual and manuscript studies. Libraries that cannot collect medieval manuscripts are often able to put together a facsimile collection that may well cover a wider range of styles, genres and historical periods than many smaller collections of original manuscripts. Facsimiles are also bought, admired, loved and studied by the amateur, the private owner, the student and the lover of the Middle Ages. They are a good example of our claim that there are many productive continuities in medievalist readerly and scholarly practice. Facsimiles are used both inside and beyond the institutional borders of the library and the university. Most professional medievalists, even those who specialise in manuscript studies, don't handle the original manuscripts they study on a daily basis. Even if their final work cites the manuscript in its archival home, a facsimile (or increasingly, an online digital image) has often played a key role in the research. If there *is* a difference in the social circumstances of facsimile use, the amateur reader or private owner may even have an advantage of proximity and intimacy in the touch of the page. Manuscript facsimiles vary widely in their rarity and expense, of course, but the most expensive, when held in libraries and museums, are sometimes treated with the same care and curatorial attentiveness as original archives. The scholar or student may still have to read and work under the disciplinary and institutional surveillance of the librarian. By contrast, the private owner or collector, whether professionally trained or not, is able to touch, handle and even write on their own copy. Most of all, the facsimile allows the individual to own, to domesticate, to touch and to display a more or less affordable piece of the exotic medieval, through the same love and desire for the medieval fulfilled by the thousands of tea towels, replicas of jewellery, stained glass, carved bosses, books, facsimiles, and key rings sold to a variety of budgets in gallery, library, and art museum shops around the world.

In their intricate and artificial materiality, facsimiles combine the modern technological sophistication of accurate reproduction with the sensory, affective appeal of the medieval. The Patrimonio company is a good example, producing many facsimiles of European manuscripts. The by-line on their website is 'The only company which uses pure gold and true precious stones for its facsimiles of the most beautiful manuscripts in the world'.[11] Their website describes the *Très Riches Heures of the Duc de Berry* in the inflated language of glamorous medievalism as 'the King of Illuminated Manuscripts', and alludes to the mysteries of their specialist expertise in language that combines the vocabulary of scholarly – medieval – work and that of the commercial patent: 'our necessary and exclusive secret process of medieval ageing'.[12] The term for their handcrafted 'pergamenata' paper invokes the learned world of Latinate parchment, and to capture its rarity value, we are told it is ten times more expensive than normal paper. Most intriguing in this context is the appeal to the senses:

> Sense of touch: absolutely similar; sense of hearing: characteristic sound while passing its folios; sense of sight: undulation and roughness similar to the folios of the original codex; sense of smell: characteristic smell.[13]

In a discussion of earlier facsimiles of the *Très Riches Heures of the Duc de Berry*, Michael Camille had, in fact, made the point that early facsimiles of the book had only been visually convincing – a product of modernity's obsession with photography and the purely ocular.[14] The professional medievalist, of course, may scorn this reproduction of smell, touch and hearing, but we think most will have experienced something of this thrill the first time they opened a medieval manuscript previously familiar only through print, microfilm or digital image, and marvelled at the discernible contrast between the smooth inner and the stippled outer side of the animal skin parchment, or the surprising thickness of medieval paper, and smelled the characteristic musty aroma of the medieval book. Moreover, this *quidditas* – the *whatness* – of the medieval manuscript sits behind many a medieval scholar's insistence to various grant bodies that a research trip to the archive is necessary, in spite of the availability of a printed facsimile or digitised version of the manuscript in question. To minimise any sense that these reproductions are cheapened or diminished through their multiplicity, the Patrimonio imprint is limited, and copies are numbered. Their facsimiles also bear the touch of the human hands that applied the 22.25 carat gold leaf illuminations, themselves further layered with 'an ageing patina and subtle micro detachments, due to the passing of centuries and currently noticeable in all medieval illuminated manuscripts'.[15]

This discourse artfully conflates modern technology and temporal progression. The medieval and the medievalist are held together in the suspension that is typical of the medievalist imaginary: the 'detachments' of gold leaf promise to replicate not just the original manuscript or its current state, but the ageing process itself. Buyers can thus experience not just a simple historical thrill of seeming to touch the past by the immediate transportation *into* the past; they can also touch the 'noticeable' passing of time through a speeded-up process that is recoded here as painstaking and slow. Medievalist objects may be new, or of recent making, but they often carry with them the potential for affective or imaginative time travel for consumers.

This is not to say that one is completely content with 'reproductions' of the Middle Ages. Walter Benjamin famously claimed that copies of the work of art inevitably denatured the original, saying 'that which withers in the age of mechanical reproduction is the aura of the work of art'.[16] Camille quotes Benjamin with approbation but takes the stance that even if the *Très Riches*

Heures is locked away forever because the reproduction is so perfect (something that early promotional material claimed would happen), it shouldn't matter because if anything 'we should view every manuscript as an object in its own right' (even or perhaps especially copies).[17] This sounds suitably democratic and would seem to inoculate us from fetishising the idea of the origin. But the symptom, our original discontent, cannot be so easily disposed of. As any number of critics have made clear, copies don't so much damage the aura of the original as stimulate our desire for the original. And the practical dangers of being satisfied with copies (especially digital ones) have been well rehearsed.[18] At the same time, our discontent cannot be completely eased by the so-called return to the book (though we both value and have written about its materiality). The book itself is merely the expression of an idea of the work. It is, in material terms, the closest one can get to that idea, but the book often hides or obfuscates that idea by its form.[19] It is, in a sense, the first material form of work – the original copy, but still a copy. Medieval studies and medievalism both share in common a desire to get back behind these copies to the original idea or work. They do so by somewhat different means but they share a discontent that runs wide and deep.

Are we disciplinary enough?

We conclude by thinking about what role this discontent has had (and might have) in much broader discussions about disciplinarity and the future of the university. We think it is fair to say that disciplinarity has generated its own level of discontent. Some argue that the real interest of disciplinarity is to perpetuate itself. Professors train students in a particular discipline who become professors in that discipline and these professors in turn train their own students to become professors and so on and so on. In this thinking it is a system more intent on its own sustenance and reproduction than on the production of knowledge.[20] Others claim that disciplinarity and specifically the discipline of medieval studies closes us off to 'amateur' approaches to temporality that might teach us that the 'present moment is more temporally heterogeneous than academically disciplined, historically minded scholars tend to let on'.[21] And we ourselves, giving voice to our discontent, have described 'discipline in its most controlling sense [as] one of the things we find most disturbing, for it indicates an almost totalizing, almost totalitarian desire to control the extent to which the field is defined'.[22] Disciplinarity in all of these instances seems to signify things that should be abhorrent to those interested in advancing the cause of education and knowledge. Disciplinarity is something that limits us; it is a mindless beast only intent on replicating itself (much like Spenser's Error); it is a relic of the nineteenth century and potentially fascistic, promising punishment to those who would exceed its boundaries.

The alternatives to this idea of a disciplinary world inevitably define themselves in terms of prefixes to the idea of discipline itself: anti-, inter-, trans-, post- and even pre-disciplinarity have all been deployed to resolve what is seen as a problem for the modern university. With the exception of pre-disciplinarity, all seem to deal with the idea that disciplinarity is really just a holdover – a dated way of thinking about the organisation of knowledge that harks back to the nineteenth century. The goal of these various methodologies is to engage with the 'new' reality of the modern university by remaking disciplinarity itself as new. One of the oldest ways of 'making it new' is to stress the nature of interdisciplinary work. And, indeed, in 1968 interdisciplinarity seemed to possess 'liberatory potential' as one critic put it.[23] But as we all know, this potential hasn't quite been realised, because interdisciplinarity (in attempting to broach the boundaries of various disciplines) actually eliminates the great desideratum of interdisciplinarity itself, which is a kind of bumping up of one discipline against another: 'Built around a plurality of approaches and perspectives, interdisciplinarity endeavours to establish a middleground of knowledge that will prove unobjectionable to the constituencies of various university and professional communities.'[24] In other words, interdisciplinarity can provoke a quiescence – as Russ Castronovo puts it: 'the politics of interdisciplinarity often amounts to a nonpolitics, a negation whose pursuit of interpretative consensus minimizes the conflict and continuing debate that characterize' truly radical approaches to knowing and acting.[25]

Post-disciplinarity would seem to offer a bit more hope. As originally conceived it was methodologically eclectic, boundary-crossing and post-professional. Its presupposition was that sanctioned modes of inquiry didn't matter because we had moved beyond them.[26] In a purely abstract way, this post-disciplinary, post-university world looks quite exciting. If we embrace the idea of post-disciplinarity as something produced in the utopic/dystopic ruin of the university, we may enjoy a collective frisson in the destruction of traditional modes of knowledge, even an obscene delight in creative destruction. But what would happen if we embraced this death wish and took a plunge into the abyss of no future? This may be a bit too exciting, however, if it means becoming part of an academic structure that might see the ruin as a perfect laboratory in which to build a corporate creature modelled on economically pragmatic lines. As Louis Menand suggests, administrators would 'love to melt down the disciplines, since that would allow universities to deploy faculty more *efficiently* [our emphasis]. Why support medievalists in the history department, the English department, the French and German departments and the art history department ... when you can hire one supermedievalist and install her in a Medieval Studies program, whose survival can be made to depend in part on its ability to attract outside funding?'[27]

As Aranye Fradenburg points out, whatever country we work in, we work increasingly in a world defined by agreements like the Bologna Declaration, which proclaims that universities across Europe should 'facilitate migration for education by homogenizing their programs of study in order to create a system of easily readable and comparable degrees ... in order to promote European citizens [sic] employability [and mobility] ... The degree awarded after the first cycle shall also be relevant to the European labor market as an appropriate level of qualification.'[28] Astonishingly, this bit of bureaucratic rhetoric actually outlines what might be our not too distant future.

Perhaps not so strangely, representatives of broader culture have especially targeted medievalists as being out of step with the 'new' university. In what has now become a seminal moment, British Education Secretary Charles Clarke mused, 'I don't mind there being some medievalists around for ornamental purposes, but there is no reason for the state to pay for them'.[29] Clarke's dismissal of medievalists as the decorative houseplant of the modern state indicates a fundamental misunderstanding of the study of medieval history and culture. But medievalists of all stripes were especially concerned when the government minister for education felt able to attack a specific educational programme on the basis of irrelevance. Both medievalists and columnists responded swiftly to Clarke, claiming both that the notion of ornament was not so easily to be dismissed and that knowledge of the medieval was essential to the creation of the responsible citizen of the modern state.[30] Events that followed showed that the implications of Clarke's comments, and others like them, were not confined simply to medievalists. Those who trotted out such easy dismissals of our discipline probably had a broader agenda in mind that embraced most of the humanities. Indeed, as became clear later, it was not just medievalists, but a certain conception of community, that Clarke was challenging. In clarifying his comments he argued, 'the medieval concept of a community of scholars seeking truth is not in itself a justification for the state to put money into that'.[31] This seems a straightforward enough (if somewhat short-sighted and ham-handed) rejection of epistemology, but Clarke also seems to be answering a question that nobody has asked. 'Medieval concept of a community of scholars? Where did that come from?'

Part of the answer might lie in Bill Readings's prescient book, *The University in Ruins*. In it he avers 'that the twilight of modernity makes the premodern a crucial site for understanding what a non-Enlightenment structure of thought might look like' – a structure that he thinks might offer some hope for the re-formation of the university.[32] For Readings, this temporal site – at once a locus of extinction and renewal, outside present structures of thought *and* fundamentally recoverable – begins to possess attributes that look very much like an earlier formulation that was used to good effect by Paul Goodman at Berkeley in the 1960s to defend the free speech movement and argued 'for a renewal of the medieval conception of the university as a "community of scholars" capable of governing itself and resisting outside forces'.[33]

The idea of a medieval conception of a community of scholars is appealing (even flattering), but it is worth examining how Readings actually characterises this community. Readings, of course, cannot escape the historical fact that the medieval university was a place where great feuds developed, 'particularly at Paris between the faculties of arts and theology and between the secular clergy and members of the mendicant orders', but he also asserts that 'the medieval University as a society for the study of knowledge was a corporate community, in the medieval sense like a guild'.[34] Some might dismiss Readings's analysis of the Middle Ages as a kind of melancholic fantasy, or quasi-Marxist nostalgia, in which 'personal dependence form[ed] the groundwork of society', and the abrupt change came when 'the guild-masters were pushed on one side' by the rise of capital. But is this all it is?[35]

To get disciplinary for just a moment, we may ask, what did this community of scholars actually look like? And why is it regarded with such suspicion by the government and such hope by academics? The great power of the university was, of course, embodied in its corporate nature. Their members 'elected their own officials and set the rules for the teaching craft ... each faculty elected its own head and held its own assemblies'.³⁶ Its power devolved from its ability to act corporately in its own interests. To give one famous example – during the carnival of 1228–9 a group of students in Bourg of S. Marcel entered a tavern and 'by chance found good and sweet wine there'.³⁷ There was a dispute with the landlord about how much they owed. A fight broke out, and the innkeeper called in his neighbours who severely beat the students. The next day, the students returned with reinforcements – they broke into the tavern, avenged themselves on the innkeeper, opened the taps and sallied forth into the streets. In the meantime, the Prior of S. Marcel had complained to the papal legate and the bishop who urged upon the regent, Blanche of Castile, the suppression of the riot. The mercenary bodyguard were called out and they attacked not the rioters themselves, but (if we can trust Matthew Paris) a group of innocent students engaged in holiday games outside the walls. A number of these students were killed. The masters of the university suspended their lectures and complained to the bishop and the legate but to no avail. On Easter Monday, the masters resolved that if they did not get justice within a month, they would dissolve the university for the period of six years and would not return until then even if they did receive redress. Ultimately most of the scholars left Paris to travel to Toulouse, Orleans, Reims and Angers and stayed away until 1231 when they apparently did get justice partially through intervention by the Pope. They were also granted a series of privileges that effectively limited the power of the bishop and the chancellor over the masters.

Over fifty years ago the Columbia historian, public intellectual and former communist Richard Hofstader used this example in his book-length treatment of academic freedom. Responding to investigations of American universities by the House Committee on Un-American Activities and a notorious case involving the dismissal of a Columbia anthropology lecturer (Gene Weltfish) for invoking the fifth amendment, he argued that the origin of academic freedom lay in the ability of faculties to act as a corporate entity. This corporate entity existed and maintained its power, he argued, only as long as it remained disciplined and enforced the disciplines. Depending on the work of the unconventional medieval scholar Mary Martin McLaughlin, he argues:

> The very solidarity of the masters in such instances suggests more than *esprit de corps* – it suggests discipline. If masters were

to undertake a cessation of lectures or migration in a body, if an entire university, or at least a faculty of theology or canon law, was to render corporate judgments on vital issues, some internal regime that would encourage if not compel agreement was necessary ... Every corporate unit of the University of Paris, for instance ... the colleges, and the separate faculties – adopted statutes and ordinances affecting almost every conceivable facet of academic life, from trivial details of dress to the subjects and methods of lectures and disputations.[38]

Most of us are a long way from enforcing sumptuary laws, or telling our colleagues what their daily lectures should contain. But we suggest it is still true that the disciplines and specifically the discipline of medieval studies not only provide us with a method to understand the past (the so-called search for truth), but also suggest a way in which that past might gesture to a future.

The idea of a discipline still holds pragmatic force. Taking Readings's view of what a future university might look like, even proponents of post-disciplinarity suggest 'not a generalized inter-disciplinary space but a certain rhythm of disciplinary attachment and detachment, which is designed so as not to let the question of disciplinarity disappear, sink into routine. Rather, disciplinary structures would be forced to answer to the name of Thought, to imagine what kinds of thinking they make possible, and what kinds of thinking they exclude.'[39] These proponents suggest 'holding on to our disciplinary objects and methods and ways of knowing, while also keeping them open to futurity and the surprise of the stranger'.[40]

If our goal is, as Fradenburg suggests, that 'people ought ... to be allowed to explore for themselves what they want to learn, teach, be, and do' (and note that her formulation includes teachers *and* students), then we have to acknowledge that the root of this freedom actually resides to a certain degree in discipline and the disciplines.[41] It is no accident that during times of crisis in the academy (the McCarthy witch-hunts of the fifties, the campus unrest of the sixties and our current crises around democracy, international relations and the role of journalism, to name just a few) the idea of the medieval community of scholars reappears, either as the utopian desideratum for academics, or for those interested in restricting intellectual freedom, as an irrelevant piece of nostalgia. There is nothing quite as terrifying to administrators and politicians as disciplined faculty resistance to external pressures because it makes transparent what should be blazingly obvious – that without academic teachers there is no university. This is why they so often cry foul, saying that we are the ones who are intolerant of dissent, that we are nothing more than an academic echo chamber, that we don't understand the best interests of the university and so on.

This is not to suggest that we should deploy the disciplines like some massive immobile Maginot line. This would be to fall into the administrators' trap of coding 'traditional' disciplines as reified 'disciplines' when, in fact, the disciplines have always been able to mobilise precisely because they are mobile (even if some of us would like to enhance this mobility just a bit). But time is short. With tenured and tenure-track positions on the decline and administrative positions on the rise there soon may not be enough with the freedom to make the question 'are we disciplinary enough?' a meaningful one.

Conclusions

Are there any? One of the most painful things we have discovered as we were writing and rewriting this book is that the ground was shifting quickly beneath us and around us, on different continents and in different contexts. Terminologies changed and took on different resonances; new scholarly voices emerged; some institutions changed, while others did not; and new collective and collaborative forms of scholarship and intellectual community rendered some of our starting propositions less urgent. To summarise the state of play as we finish this book (this version; this final manuscript; this copy-edited text; these proofs) would provoke disagreement, disavowal and denial. This changing state of affairs is not unique to our field, of course: instead, we suggest it is symptomatic of the contemporary humanities. Where so much is at stake – such competition for shrinking resources – such dissent, and such powerful feelings, are inevitable.

However, we think that medieval and medievalism studies are well placed to model new forms of engagement. By this we mean something very different from the older, somewhat reluctant and often patronising concession by old-school medieval scholars that the modern enthusiasm for medievalism in popular culture might serve as a kind of lure to attract students into the field of medieval philology and history. Instead, our final suggestion is that we actively embrace the proliferation of terms that have entangled many commentators, between medieval and medievalism, as well as neomedievalism, post-medievalism, the medievalist and all the others. What if we were to let go of those hard-won but ultimately unsuccessful distinctions, and accept that they serve only to divide us from each other? What if we were to redefine *all* of those things as performing essentially the same work: that is, helping us to imagine our future as well as reading our past. We might all start, then, by being discontent with both medievalism and medieval studies, for a variety of reasons: because they are not medieval enough; or because they do the medieval, or medievalism, the wrong way; or because the medieval has come to mean the wrong thing. Such discontent, however, borne out of love, is our best way forward to future collective and productive dialogue with the past.

Notes

1 Freud, *Civilization and Its Discontents*, p. 149.
2 Matthews makes the case for medievalism's ongoing dialogue with cultural studies in the conclusion to *Medievalism: A Critical History*.
3 Baudrillard, *Simulacra and Simulation*, p. 2.
4 Watson, 'Touring the medieval', p. 255. For the pervasive recent influence of Baudrillard see Fitzpatrick, '(Re)producing (neo)medievalism', p. 17, n. 2.
5 Mayer, 'Simulacrum', p. 223.
6 Baudrillard, *Simulacra and Simulation*, p. 2.
7 Baudrillard, *Simulacra and Simulation*, p. 6. Baudrillard makes himself even clearer later when he claims, 'history thus made its triumphal entry into cinema, posthumously (the term historical has undergone the same fate: a "historical" moment, monument, congress, figure are in this way designated as fossils). Its reinjection has no value as conscious awareness but only as nostalgia for a lost referential' (*Simulacra and Simulation*, p. 44).
8 For a recent example of this kind of reading see Trilling, 'Medievalism and its discontents', pp. 216–24.
9 This is Paul de Man's characterisation. Qtd in Kuskin, *Recursive Origins*, p. 44.
10 Kuskin, *Recursive Origins*, p. 44.
11 http://patrimonio-ediciones.com/en/facsimile/, accessed 27 June 2017.
12 http://patrimonio-ediciones.com.mialias.net/en/facsimil/the-tres-riches-heures-of-the-duke-of-berry, accessed 22 February 2013. 'First, true and unique fine facsimile edition with pergamenata paper specially treated. This exclusive handcrafted paper which price is 10 times superior to couche paper, used by Patrimonio in their commentary volumes, enables you, after our necessary and exclusive secret process of medieval ageing, to enjoy the following senses.'
13 http://patrimonio-ediciones.com/en/facsimile/, accessed 27 June 2017.

14 Camille, 'The *très riches heures*', pp. 103–4.
15 http://patrimonio-ediciones.com/en/facsimile/, accessed 27 June 2017.
16 Benjamin, 'The work of art', pp. 219–53.
17 Camille, 'The *très riches heures*', p. 74.
18 See Edwards's 'Back to the real?' for a concise rehearsal of this argument.
19 See Smith's invocation of Blanchot above (p. 102). As Smith points out, some believe that the work cannot be separated from its material form.
20 Menand, *The Marketplace of Ideas*, p. 105.
21 Dinshaw, *How Soon Is Now?*, p. ix.
22 Prendergast and Trigg, 'What is happening to the Middle Ages?', pp. 215–29.
23 See Castronovo, 'Within the veil of interdisciplinary knowledge?', p. 781.
24 Castronovo, 'Within the veil of interdisciplinary knowledge?', p. 784.
25 Castronovo, 'Within the veil of interdisciplinary knowledge?', p. 784.
26 Menand, *The Marketplace of Ideas*, p. 87.
27 Menand, *The Marketplace of Ideas*, p. 105.
28 Fradenburg, *Staying Alive*, p. 9.
29 Smithers and Woodward, 'Clarke dismisses medieval historians'. After a good deal of criticism, Clarke, in a letter to the *Guardian* of 10 May 2003, attempted to explain what he meant, saying 'My use of the word "medieval" in this context has obviously been somehow transformed into a criticism of the study of medievalism in all its forms, which is not at all what I think.' Interestingly, in a discussion of university fees, he had earlier dismissed Classics (though not Philosophy).
30 The responses were many, but see Lightfoot, 'Medieval study "is history"'.
31 'Clarke questions study'.
32 Readings, *The University in Ruins*, p. 226.
33 Johnson et al. (eds), *Steal This University*, p. 11.
34 Readings, *The University in Ruins*, p. 181.
35 Marx, Capital, 1, p. 50; Marx, The Communist Manifesto, p. 15.
36 Hofstader, *Academic Freedom*, p. 6.
37 Rashdall, *The Universities of Europe in the Middle Ages*, vol. 1, p. 334.
38 Hofstader, *Academic Freedom*, p. 10.
39 Readings, *The University in Ruins*, p. 176.
40 Babel Working Group, 'Cruising in the ruins'.
41 Fradenburg, *Staying Alive*, p. 13.

Bibliography

Primary sources

Ælfric's Catholic Homilies: The Second Series, ed. Malcolm C. Godden, Early English Text Society, s.s. 5, London: Oxford University Press, 1979.

Ascham, Roger, Toxophilus, ed. Edward Arber, London: Murray, 1868.

Augustine, Saint, On Christian Doctrine, trans. D. W. Robertson, Jr., Indianapolis: Bobbs-Merrill, 1958.

Augustine, Saint, Confessions, trans. Henry Chadwick, Oxford: Oxford University Press, 1998.

Barnes, Julian, The Sense of an Ending, New York: Alfred A. Knopf, 2011.

Bergman, Ingmar (dir.), The Seventh Seal, Svensk Filmindustri, 1957.

Boccaccio, Giovanni, The Decameron, ed. and trans. G. H. McWilliams, New York: Penguin, 1995.

The Book of Margery Kempe, ed. Barry Windeatt, Woodbridge: D. S. Brewer, 2006.

Chaucer, Geoffrey, Troilus and Criseyde, in Larry D. Benson (gen. ed.), The Riverside Chaucer, 3rd edn, Oxford: Oxford University Press, 1987.

'Constantine the Great, the empress Helena and the relics of the holy cross', ed. and trans. E. Gordon Whatley, in Thomas Head (ed.), Medieval Hagiography: An Anthology, New York: Routledge, 2001, 77–97.

Dunbar, William, 'Lament for the makirs', in Douglas Gray (ed.), The Oxford Book of Late Medieval Verse and Prose, Oxford: Oxford University Press, 1985.

Einhard, The Translations and Miracles of the Blessed Martyrs, Marcellinus and Peter, in Peter Edward Dutton (ed.), Charlemagne's Courtier: The Complete Einhard, Peterborough: Broadview, 1998, 69–91.

Freud, Sigmund, Civilization and Its Discontents, trans. James Strachey, New York: W. W. Norton & Co., 2005.

Freud, Sigmund, The Complete Letters of Sigmund Freud to Wilhelm Fliess, 1887–1904, ed. and trans. J. M. Masson, Cambridge, MA: Harvard University Press, 1985.

Gildas, The Ruin of Britain and Other Works, ed. and trans. Michael Winterbottom, London: Phillimore, 1978.

Bibliography

Green, Monica H. (ed.), *The Trotula: A Medieval Compendium of Women's Medicine*, Philadelphia: University of Pennsylvania Press, 2001.

Guibert de Nogent, *Treatise on Relics*, in C. G. Coulton (ed.), *Life in the Middle Ages*, vol. 1, New York: Macmillan, c.1910, 15–22, http://sourcebooks.fordham.edu/source/nogent-relics.asp. Accessed 20 June 2017.

Harvey, John, *A Discursive Probleme Concerninge Prophesies*, London, 1588.

Julian of Norwich, *The Writings of Julian of Norwich: A Vision Showed to a Devout Woman and a Revelation of Her Love*, ed. Nicholas Watson and Jacqueline Jenkins, University Park: Pennsylvania State University, 2006.

Kempe, Margery, *The Book of Margery Kempe*, ed. Barry Windeatt, Cambridge: D. S. Brewer, 2004.

Langland, William, *Piers Plowman: The C Version*, ed. George Russell and George Kane, London: Athlone; Berkeley and Los Angeles: University of California Press, 1997.

Marx, Karl, Capital: *A Critique of Political Economy*, ed. Frederick Engels, trans. Samuel Moore and Edward Aveling, Moscow, 1887.

Marx, Karl and Frederick Engels, *The Communist Manifesto*, trans. Samuel Moore, New York: Bantam Dell, 2004.

Morris, William, *A Dream of John Ball and a King's Lesson*, New York: Longmans, Green & Co., 1903.

Morris, William, *News from Nowhere: Or, an Epoch of Rest, Being Some Chapters from a Utopian Romance*, London: Kelmscott Press, 1892.

Poems, supposed to have been written at Bristol, by Thomas Rowley, and others, in the fifteenth century; the greatest part now first published from the most authentic copies, with an engraved specimen of one of the mss., ed. Thomas Tyrwhitt, London, 1777.

Raymond of Capua, *The Life of Catherine of Siena*, trans. and intro. Conleth Kearns, Dublin: Dominican Publications, 1980.

Saint Erkenwald, ed. Clifford Peterson, Philadelphia: University of Pennsylvania Press, 1977.

A Select Library of Nicene and Post-Nicene Fathers of the Christian Church, ed. and trans. Philip Schaff and Henry Wace, second series, Grand Rapids: W. B. Eerdmans Pub. Co., 1952–7.

The Shewings of Julian of Norwich, ed. Georgia Ronan Crampton, Kalamazoo: Medieval Institute Publications, 1994.

Sir Orfeo, ed. Anne Laskaya and Eve Salisbury, *The Middle English Breton Lays*, TEAMS Middle English Texts Series, http://d.lib.rochester.edu/teams/text/laskaya-and-salisbury-middle-english-breton-lays-sir-orfeo.

Spenser, Edmund, *The Faerie Queene*, ed. Thomas P. Roche Jr. with the assistance of C. Patrick O'Donnell Jr., New Haven: Yale University Press, 1981.

Spielberg, Steven (dir.), *Raiders of the Lost Ark*, Paramount / Lucasfilm, 1981.

Tarantino, Quentin (dir.), *Pulp Fiction*, Miramax, 1994.
Tyrwhitt, Thomas (ed.), *The Canterbury Tales of Chaucer to which are added, an essay upon his language and versification; an introductory discourse; and notes*, London, 1775–8.
Wells, H. G. *The Time Machine*, New York: Dover Publications, 1995.
Voragine, Jacobi a. *Legenda aurea: vulgo Historia lombardica dicta* ad optimorum librorum fidem recensuit Th. Graesse. 3 ed., Breslau: Koebner, 1890.

Secondary works

Alexander, Michael, *Medievalism: The Middle Ages in Modern England*, New Haven and London: Yale University Press, 2007.
Alipaz, Daniel, 'Merleau-Ponty's Bergson', *Philament*, 18 (2012), 66–83.
Altschul, Nadia, 'Transfer', in Elizabeth Emery and Richard Utz (eds), *Medievalism: Key Critical Terms*, Cambridge: D. S. Brewer, 2014, 239–45.
Aronstein, Susan, *Hollywood Knights: Arthurian Cinema and the Politics of Nostalgia*, New York: Palgrave Macmillan, 2005.
Aston, Margaret, 'English ruins and English history: the dissolution and the sense of the past', *Journal of the Warburg and Courtauld Institutes*, 36 (1973), 231–55.
Babel Working Group, 'Cruising in the ruins: the question of disciplinarity in the post/medieval university', http://babel-meeting.org/2012-meeting.org/. Accessed 28 April 2014.
Bachrach, Bernard S., '*A Distant Mirror: The Calamitous 14th Century* by Barbara W. Tuchman: a review', *American Historical Review*, 84:3 (1979), 724–5.
Baker, Donald C., 'Frederick James Furnivall (1825–1910)', in Paul Ruggiers (ed.), *Editing Chaucer: The Great Tradition*, Norman: Pilgrim Books, 1984, 157–69.
Baldick, Chris, *The Oxford Book of Gothic Tales*, Oxford: Oxford University Press, 2009.
Battles, Dominique, '*Sir Orfeo* and English identity', *Studies in Philology*, 107 (2010), 179–211.
Baudrillard, Jean, *Simulacra and Simulation*, trans. Sheila Faria Glaser, Ann Arbor: University of Michigan Press, 1994.
Bell, Rudolph, *Holy Anorexia*, Chicago: University of Chicago Press, 1985.
Benjamin, Walter, 'The work of art in the age of mechanical reproduction', in Hannah Arendt (ed.), *Illuminations*, New York: Harcourt, Brace and World, 1968, 219–53.
Bennett, Jane, *Vibrant Matter: A Political Ecology of Things*, Durham: Duke University Press, 2010.
Bergson, Henri, *Matière et mémoire: Essai sur la relation du corps à l'esprit*, Paris: Les presses universitaires de France, 1965.

Bibliography

Bestul, Thomas, 'Antecedents: the Anselmian and Cistercian contributions', in William F. Pollard and Robert Boenig (eds), *Mysticism and Spirituality in Medieval England*, Cambridge: D. S. Brewer, 1997, 1–21.

Biddick, Kathleen, *The Shock of Medievalism*, Durham: Duke University Press, 1998.

Bildhauer, Bettina, *Filming the Middle Ages*, Chicago: Reaktion Books, 2011.

Binski, Paul, *Medieval Death: Ritual and Representation*, Ithaca: Cornell University Press, 1996.

Boyd, J. T., 'Labor and revolt in Mark Twain and William Morris', *Nineteenth-Century Prose*, 42 (2015), 73–94.

Brewer, Derek, *Chaucer: The Critical Heritage*, London: Routledge, 1978.

Brewer, Keagan, *Wonder and Skepticism in the Middle Ages*, New York: Routledge, 2016.

Bronfen, Elisabeth, *Over Her Dead Body*, New York: Routledge, 1992.

Brooks, Chris. *The Gothic Revival*, London: Phaidon, 1999.

Brown, Carleton (ed.), *Religious Lyrics of the XIVth Century*, 2nd edn, rev. G. V. Smithers, Oxford: Clarendon, 1952.

Brown, Harry, 'Baphomet incorporated: a case study in neomedievalism', *Studies in Medievalism*, 20 (2011), 1–10.

Burdick, John, *William Morris: Redesigning the World*, New York: Todtri Productions, 1997.

Burke, Peter, *The Renaissance Sense of the Past*, London: Edward Arnold, 1969.

Burrow, J. A. and Thorlac Turville-Petre, *A Book of Middle English*, 3rd edn, Oxford: Blackwell, 2005.

Bynum, Caroline Walker, *Holy Feast and Holy Fast: The Religious Significance of Food to Medieval Women*, Berkeley: University of California Press, 1988.

Bynum, Caroline Walker, 'Wonder', *American Historical Review*, 112 (1997), 1–26.

Caie, Graham and Chris Jones, 'The Middle Ages, a distant mirror: medieval life and death and medievalism through the centuries. Professor Graham Caie FRSE in conversation with Dr Chris Jones, 17 November 2010', *YouTube*, 17 June 2011, www.youtube.com/watch?v=Vceu9qXMfjA. Accessed 20 June 2017.

Camille, Michael, 'The *Très Riches Heures*: an illuminated manuscript in the age of mechanical reproduction', *Critical Inquiry*, 17:1 (1990), 72–107.

Carpenter, Humphrey, *The Inklings: C. S. Lewis, J. R. R. Tolkien and their Friends*, New York: Harper Collins, 2006.

Cartlidge, Neil, 'Sir Orfeo in the Otherworld: courting chaos?', *Studies in the Age of Chaucer*, 26 (2004), 195–226.

Castronovo, Russ, 'Within the veil of interdisciplinary knowledge? Jefferson, Du Bois and the negation of politics', *New Literary History*, 31 (2000), 781–804.

Chaganti, Seeta, 'Danse macabre and the virtual churchyard', *postmedieval*, 3 (2012), 7–26.

Chaganti, Seeta, *The Medieval Poetics of the Reliquary: Enshrinement, Inscription, Performance*, New York: Palgrave, 2008.

Chandler, Alice, *A Dream of Order: The Medieval Ideal in Nineteenth-Century English Literature*, Lincoln: University of Nebraska Press, 1970.

'Clarke questions study as "adornment"'. *BBC News*, 9 May 2003, http://news.bbc.co.uk/2/hi/uk_news/education/3014423.stm. Accessed 18 January 2012.

Clements, Pam, 'Authenticity', in Elizabeth Emery and Richard Utz (eds), *Medievalism: Key Critical Terms*, Cambridge: D. S. Brewer, 2014, 19–26.

Cohen, Jeffrey Jerome, *Of Giants: Sex, Monsters, and the Middle Ages*, Minneapolis: University of Minnesota Press, 1999.

Cohen, Jeffrey Jerome, *Medieval Identity Machines*, Minnesota: University of Minneapolis Press, 2003.

Cohen, Jeffrey Jerome (ed.), *The Postcolonial Middle Ages*, New York: Palgrave, 2000.

Cole, Andrew and D. Vance Smith (eds), *The Legitimacy of the Middle Ages*, Durham: Duke University Press, 2010.

Cramer, Michael A., *Medieval Fantasy as Performance: The Society for Creative Anachronism and the Current Middle Ages*, Lanham: Scarecrow Press, 2010.

Cunningham, Peter (ed.), *The Letters of Horace Walpole*, London: Richard Bentley and Son, 1891.

D'Arcens, Louise, *The Cambridge Companion to Medievalism*, Cambridge: Cambridge University Press, 2016.

D'Arcens, Louise, *Comic Medievalism: Laughing at the Middle Ages*, Cambridge: D. S. Brewer, 2014.

D'Arcens, Louise, *Old Songs in the Timeless Land: Medievalism in Australian Literature 1840–1910*, Turnhout: Brepols, 2011.

Davis, Kathleen, 'The sense of an epoch: periodization, sovereignty and the limits of secularization', in Andrew Cole and D. Vance Smith (eds), *The Legitimacy of the Middle Ages*, Durham: Duke University Press, 2010, 39–69.

Davis, Kathleen, 'Time behind the veil: The media, the middle ages, and orientalism now', in Jeffrey Jerome Cohen (ed.), *The Postcolonial Middle Ages*, New York: Palgrave, 2000, 105–22.

Davis, Kathleen and Nadia Altschul, 'The idea of "the Middle Ages" outside Europe', in Davis and Altschul (eds), *Medievalisms in the Postcolonial World: The Idea of 'the Middle Ages' outside Europe*, Baltimore: Johns Hopkins University Press, 2009.

Deleuze, Gilles, *The Logic of Sense*, New York: Continuum, 2005.

Deleuze, Gilles and Félix Guattari, A Thousand Plateaus: Capitalism and Schizophrenia, trans. and foreword Brian Massumi, Minneapolis: University of Minnesota Press, 1987.

Bibliography

Dinshaw, Carolyn, *Getting Medieval: Sexualities and Communities, Pre- and Postmodern*, Durham: Duke University Press, 1999.

Dinshaw, Carolyn, *How Soon Is Now? Medieval Texts, Amateur Readers, and the Queerness of Time*, Durham: Duke University Press, 2012.

Dinshaw, Carolyn, 'Nostalgia on my mind', *postmedieval*, 2:2 (2011), 225–38.

'Doctor Who in the Middle Ages', *Medievalists.Net*, 22 November 2013, www.medievalists.net/2013/11/doctor-who-in-the-middle-ages/. Accessed 12 June 2017.

Doty, Alexander and Patricia Ingham, *The Witch and the Hysteric: The Monstrous Medieval in Benjamin Christensen's Häxan*, Brooklyn: Punctum Books, 2014.

Downes, Stephanie and Rebecca F. McNamara, 'The history of emotions and Middle English literature', *Literature Compass*, 13:6 (2016), 444–56.

During, Simon, 'Literary subjectivity', *Ariel*, 31 (2000), 33–50.

Eco, Umberto, 'Dreaming of the Middle Ages', in Eco, *Faith in Fakes: Essays*, trans. William Weaver, London: Secker and Warburg, 1986, 61–72.

Eco, Umberto, 'Towards a new Middle Ages', in Marshall Blonsky (ed.), *On Signs*, Oxford: Basil Blackwell, 1985, 488–504.

Edelman, Lee, *No Future: Queer Theory and the Death Drive*, Durham: Duke University Press, 2004.

Edwards, A. S. G., 'Back to the real?', *Times Literary Supplement*, 7 June 2013, www.the-tls.co.uk/articles/public/back-to-the-real/. Accessed 20 June 2017.

Eigen, Michael, 'The annihilated self', *The Psychoanalytic Review*, 93:1 (2006), 25–38.

Eisenman, Stephen F., 'Communism in furs: a dream of prehistory in William Morris's "John Ball"', *The Art Bulletin*, 87 (2005), 92–110.

Elliot, Dyan, 'Seeing double: Jean Gerson, the discernment of spirits and Joan of Arc', *American Historical Review*, 107 (2002), 26–54.

Emery, Elizabeth and Richard Utz (eds), *Medievalism: Key Critical Terms*, Cambridge: D. S. Brewer, 2014.

Fabian, Johannes, *Time and the Other: How Anthropology Makes Its Object*, New York: Columbia University Press, 1983.

Federico, Sylvia, *New Troy: Fantasies of Empire in the Late Middle Ages*, Minneapolis: University of Minnesota Press, 2003.

Felski, Rita, *The Limits of Critique*, Chicago: University of Chicago Press, 2015.

Felski, Rita and Susan Fraiman, 'Introduction', *New Literary History*, 43 (2012), v–xii.

Ferguson, Arthur B., *Utter Antiquity: Perceptions of Prehistory in Renaissance England*, Durham: Duke University Press, 1993.

Fitzpatrick, KellyAnn, '(Re)producing (neo)medievalism', *Studies in Medievalism*, 20 (2011), 11–19.

Flatley, Jonathan, *Affective Mapping: Melancholia and the Politics of Modernism*, Cambridge, MA: Harvard University Press, 2008.

Fleming, Juliet, 'Scraping by: towards a pre-historic criticism', *postmedieval*, 3:1 (2012), 119–33.

Forni, Kathleen, *The Chaucerian Apocrypha: A Counterfeit Canon*, Gainesville: University Press of Florida, 2001.

Forni, Kathleen, *Chaucer's Afterlife: Adaptations in Recent Popular Culture*, Jefferson: McFarland & Co., 2013.

Foucault, Michel, 'Questions on geography', in Foucault, *Power/Knowledge: Selections, Interviews and Other Writings 1972–1977*, ed. and trans. Colin Gordon, New York: Vintage, 1980, 63–77.

Fradenburg, L. O. Aranye, *Sacrifice Your Love: Psychoanalysis, Historicism, Chaucer*, Minneapolis: University of Minnesota Press, 2002.

Fradenburg, L. O. Aranye, *Staying Alive: A Survival Manual for the Liberal Arts*, Brooklyn: Punctum Books, 2013.

Fradenburg, Louise O., '"Voice Memorial": loss and reparation in Chaucer's poetry', *Exemplaria*, 2 (1990), 169–202.

Freud, Sigmund, *The Standard Edition of the Complete Psychological Works of Sigmund Freud*, ed. and trans. J. Strachey, London: Hogarth Press, 1953–74.

Freud, Sigmund, *The Uncanny*, trans. David Mclintock, New York: Penguin, 2003.

Furness, Hannah, 'Hilary Mantel: women writers must stop falsely empowering female characters in history', *The Telegraph*, 31 May 2017, www.telegraph.co.uk/news/2017/05/31/hilary-mantel-women-writers-must- stop-falsely-empowering-female/. Accessed 8 June 2017.

Furnivall, F. J., A *Temporary Preface to the Six Text Edition of Chaucer's Canterbury Tales*, pt. 1 (London: 1868).

Geary, Patrick J., *Furta Sacra: Thefts of Relics in the Central Middle Ages*, rev. edn, Princeton: Princeton University Press, 1990.

Godden, Richard H., 'Getting medieval in real time', *postmedieval*, 2:3 (2011), 267–77.

Godden, Richard H., 'Nerds, love, amateurs: reflections on *How Soon Is Now?*', *Modern Medieval*, 29 March 2013, http://modernmedieval.blogspot.com.au/2013/03/nerds-love-amateurs-reflections-on-how.html. Accessed 13 January 2016.

Greg, W. W., 'Books and bookmen in the correspondence of Archbishop Parker', *The Library*, 4th series, 16 (1936), 243–79.

Hanning, Robert W., *The Vision of History in Early Britain: From Gildas to Geoffrey of Monmouth*, New York: Columbia University Press, 1966.

Haydock, Nickolas, *Movie Medievalism: The Imaginary Middle Ages*, Jefferson: McFarland & Co., 2008.

Hirsch, Marianne, 'The generation of postmemory', *Poetics Today*, 29 (2008), 103–28.

Hofstader, Richard, *Academic Freedom in the Age of the College*, New Brunswick: Transaction Publishers, 1964.

Holsinger, Bruce, 'Neomedievalism and international relations', in Louise D'Arcens (ed.), *The Cambridge Companion to Medievalism*, Cambridge: Cambridge University Press, 2016, 165–79.

Bibliography

Holsinger, Bruce, *The Premodern Condition: Medievalism and the Making of Theory*, Chicago: University of Chicago Press, 2005.

Horstman, C., *Yorkshire Writers: Richard Rolle of Hampole, a English Father of the Church and his Followers*, London: Swan Sonnenchein, 1895–6

Huizinga, Johan, *The Waning of the Middle Ages*, trans. Frederick Jan Hopman, London: Edward Arnold and Co., 1924.

Ingham, Patricia Clare, 'Amorous dispossessions: knowledge, desire, and the poet's body', in Elizabeth Scala and Sylvia Federico (eds), *The Post-Historical Middle Ages*, New York: Palgrave, 2009, 13–36.

Ingham, Patricia Clare, 'Making all things new: past, progress and the promise of utopia', *Journal of Medieval and Early Modern Studies*, 36 (2006), 479–92.

Ingham, Patricia Clare, 'Marking time: Branwen, daughter of Llyr and the colonial refrain', in Jeffrey Jerome Cohen (ed.), *The Postcolonial Middle Ages*, New York: Palgrave, 2000, 173–91.

Ingham, Patricia Clare, *The Medieval New: Ambivalence in an Age of Innovation*, Philadelphia: University of Pennsylvania Press, 2015.

Jaeger, C. Stephen, *Enchantment: On Charisma and the Sublime in the Arts of the West*, Philadelphia: University of Pennsylvania Press, 2012.

James, Paul, *Globalism, Nationalism, Tribalism: Bringing Theory Back In*, London: Sage, 2006.

Johnson, Benjamin, Patrick Kavanagh and Kevin Mattson (eds), *Steal This University: The Rise of the Corporate University and the Academic Labor Movement*, New York: Routledge, 2003.

Jones, Mike Rodman, 'Early modern medievalism', in Louise d'Arcens (ed.), *The Cambridge Companion to Medievalism*, Cambridge: Cambridge University Press, 2016, 89–102.

Joy, Eileen A., '"What counts is not to say, but to say again": a response to Thomas A. Bredehoft, "Anglo-Saxonists and eBay"', *Old English Newsletter*, 37:3 (2004), 25–30.

Justice, Steven, 'Did the Middle Ages believe in their miracles?' *Representations*, 103 (2008), 1–29.

Kane, George, *Middle English Literature: A Critical Study of the Romances, the Religious Lyrics, Piers Plowman*, London: Methuen, 1951.

Kinch, Ashby, *Imago Mortis: Mediating Images of Death in Late Medieval Culture*, Leiden: Brill, 2013.

King, Andrew, *The Faerie Queene and Middle English Romance: The Matter of Just Memory*, Oxford: Clarendon Press, 2000.

Klein, Kerwin Lee, 'On the emergence of *memory* in historical discourse', *Representations*, 69 (2000), 127–50.

Koopman, Rachel, *Wonderful to Relate: Miracle Stories and Miracle Collecting in High Medieval England*, Philadelphia: University of Pennsylvania, 2010.

Kuskin, William, *Recursive Origins: Writing at the Transition to Modernity*, Notre Dame: University of Notre Dame Press, 2013.

Latour, Bruno, *We Have Never Been Modern*, trans. Catherine Porter, Cambridge, MA: Harvard University Press, 1993.

Lepore, Jill, 'The dark ages: terrorism, counterterrorism, and law of torment', *The New Yorker*, 28 March 2013, 1–32.

Lerer, Seth, 'Artifice and artistry in *Sir Orfeo*', *Speculum*, 60 (1985), 92–109.

Lerer, Seth, *Chaucer and His Readers: Imagining the Author in Late-Medieval England*, Princeton: Princeton University Press, 1993.

Lerer, Seth, *Error and the Academic Self: The Scholarly Imagination, Medieval to Modern*, New York: Columbia University Press, 2002.

Levine, J. M., *Humanism and History: Origins of Modern English Historiography*, Ithaca: Cornell University Press, 1987.

Lewis, W. S. (ed.), *The Yale Edition of Horace Walpole's Correspondence*, New Haven: Yale University Press, 1937–83.

Lightfoot, Liz, 'Medieval study "is history"', *Daily Telegraph* (5 September 2003).

Lindley, Arthur C., 'The ahistoricism of medieval film', *Screening the Past*, 3 (1998), www.screeningthepast.com/2014/12/the-ahistoricism-of-medieval-film/. Accessed 3 July 2017.

Lochrie, Karma, *Margery Kempe and the Translations of the Flesh*, Philadelphia: University of Pennsylvania Press, 1994.

Loud, G. A., 'Monastic chronicles in the twelfth-century Abruzzi', *Anglo-Norman Studies*, 27 (2004), 101–26.

Lukes, Daniel, 'Comparative neomedievalisms: a little bit medieval', *postmedieval*, 5:1 (2013), 1–9.

Maidment, Paul, 'Islamic finance: a distant mirror', *Forbes* (21 April 2008), www.forbes.com/2008/04/21/christian-islamic-usury-islamic-finance-islamicfinance08-cx_pm_0421medieval.html. Accessed 20 June 2017.

Malo, Robyn, *Relics and Writing in Late Medieval England*, Toronto: University of Toronto Press, 2013.

Mann, Jill, 'Troilus' swoon', *Chaucer Review*, 14 (1980), 319–35.

Manning, Stephen, *Wisdom and Number: Toward a Critical Appraisal of the Middle English Religious Lyric*, Lincoln: University of Nebraska Press, 1962.

Mannoni, Octave, 'I know well, but all the same ...', in Molly Anne Rothenberg, Dennis A. Foster and Slavoj Žižek (eds), *Perversion and the Social Relation*, Durham: Duke University Press, 2003, 68–92.

Marshall, David W., 'Neomedievalism, identification and the haze of medievalisms', *Studies in Medievalism*, 20 (2011), 21–34.

Marshall, Peter, 'Forgery and miracles in the reign of Henry VIII', *Past and Present*, 178 (2003), 39–73.

Massey, Doreen, *For Space*, London: Sage Publications, 2005.

Matthews, David, 'Chaucer's American accent', *American Literary History*, 22:4 (2010), 758–71.

Matthews, David, *The Making of Middle English: 1765–1910*, Minneapolis: Minnesota University Press, 1999.

Matthews, David, *Medievalism: A Critical History*, Cambridge: D. S. Brewer, 2015.

Matthews, David, 'What was medievalism? Medieval studies, medievalism and cultural studies', in Ruth Evans, Helen Fulton and David

Matthews (eds), *Medieval Cultural Studies: Essays in Honour of Stephen Knight*, Cardiff: University of Wales Press, 2006, 9–22.

McGurk, J. J. N., 'A Distant Mirror (book review)', *History Today*, 29 (1979), 412–13.

McNamer, Sarah, *Affective Meditation and the Invention of Medieval Compassion*, Philadelphia, University of Pennsylvania Press, 2010.

Mayer, Lauryn S, 'Simulation', in Elizabeth Emery and Richard Utz (eds), *Medievalism: Key Critical Terms*, Cambridge: D. S. Brewer, 2014, 223–30.

Menand, Louis, *The Marketplace of Ideas: Reform and Resistance in the American University*, New York: W. W. Norton, 2010.

Miller, Joseph Hillis, *Literature as Conduct: Speech Acts in Henry James*, New York: Fordham University Press, 2005.

Miskimin, Alice, 'The illustrated eighteenth-century Chaucer', *Modern Philology*, 77 (1979), 26–55.

Mitford, Rev. John (ed.), *The Correspondence of Horace Walpole, Earl of Oxford: and the Reverend William Mason*, London: Richard Bentley, 1851.

Morris, William, 'Paper read at the seventh annual meeting of the SPAB, 1 July, 1884', in May Morris (ed.), *William Morris: Artist, Writer, Socialist*, Oxford: Basil Blackwell, 1936, vol. 1, 124–45.

Munro, John (ed.), *Frederick James Furnivall: A Volume of Personal Record*, London: Frowde, 1911.

Nagy, Piroska and Damien Bouquet, *Sensible Moyen Age: Une histoire d'émotions dans l'Occident medieval*, Paris: Seuil, 2015.

Newman, Barbara, *God and Goddesses: Vision Poetry and Belief in the Middle Ages*, Philadelphia: University of Pennsylvania Press, 2005.

Nora, Pierre, 'Between memory and history: les lieux de mémoire', *Representations*, 26 (1989), 7–24.

Otter, Monika, '"New Werke": St. Erkenwald, St. Albans, and the medieval sense of the past', *Journal of Medieval and Renaissance Studies*, 24 (1994), 387–415.

Patterson, Lee, *Negotiating the Past: The Historical Understanding of Medieval Literature*, Madison: University of Wisconsin Press, 1987.

Patterson, Lee, 'On the margin: postmodernism, ironic history, and medieval studies', *Speculum*, 65 (1990), 87–108.

Pearsall, Derek, 'Interpretive models for the Peasants' Revolt', in Patrick J. Gallacher and Helen Damico (eds), *Hermeneutics and Medieval Culture*, Albany: State University of New York Press, 1989, 63–70.

Pearsall, Derek, 'Madness in *Sir Orfeo*', in Jennifer Fellows, Rosalind Field, Gilliam Rogers and Judith Weiss (eds), *Romance Reading on the Book: Essays in Medieval Narrative Presented to Maldwyn Mills*, Cardiff: University of Wales Press, 1996, 51–63.

Powell, L. F., 'Thomas Tyrwhitt and the Rowley poems', *RES*, 7 (1931), 314–26.

Prendergast, Thomas A., 'Canon formation', in Marion Turner (ed.), *A Handbook of Middle English Studies*, Chichester: Wiley-Blackwell, 2013, 239–51.

Prendergast, Thomas A., *Chaucer's Dead Body: From Corpse to Corpus*, New York: Routledge, 2004.
Prendergast, Thomas A. and Stephanie Trigg, 'The negative erotics of medievalism', in Elizabeth Scala and Sylvia Federico (eds), *The Post-Historical Middle Ages*, Basingstoke: Palgrave Macmillan, 2010, 117–38.
Prendergast, Thomas A. and Stephanie Trigg, 'What is happening to the Middle Ages?', *New Medieval Literatures*, 9 (2008), 215–29.
Pugh, Tison and Angela Jane Weisl, *Medievalisms: Making the Past in the Present*, London and New York: Routledge, 2013.
Rashdall, Hastings, *The Universities of Europe in the Middle Ages*, 3 vols, ed. and rev. A. B. Emden and Sir Maurice Powicke, Oxford: Oxford University Press, 1936.
Readings, Bill, *The University in Ruins*, Cambridge, MA: Harvard University Press, 1996.
Reiss, Edmund, *The Art of the Middle English Lyric: Essays in Criticism*, Athens: University of Georgia Press, 1972.
Riddy, Felicity, 'The uses of the past in *Sir Orfeo*', *The Yearbook of English Studies*, 6 (1976), 5–15.
Rider, Jeff, 'Receiving Orpheus in the Middle Ages: allegorization, remythification and *Sir Orfeo*', *Papers on Language and Literature*, 24 (1988), 343–66.
Robertson, D. W., Jr., *A Preface to Chaucer: Studies in Medieval Perspectives*, Princeton: Princeton University Press, 1962.
Robinson, Carol L. and Pamela Clements, 'Living with neomedievalism', *Studies in Medievalism*, 18 (2009), 55–75.
Rosenwein, Barbara (ed.), *Anger's Past: The Social Uses of an Emotion in the Middle Ages*, Ithaca: Cornell University Press, 1998.
Rosenwein, Barbara, *Emotional Communities in the Early Middle Ages*, Ithaca: Cornell University Press, 2006.
Rosenwein, Barbara, *Generations of Feeling: A History of Emotions 600–1700*, Cambridge: Cambridge University Press, 2006.
Rouse, Margitta, 'Rethinking anachronism for medieval film in Richard Donner's *Timeline*', in Andrew James Johnston, Margitta Rouse and Philipp Hinz (eds), *The Medieval Motion Picture: The Politics of Adaptation*, New York: Palgrave Macmillan, 2014, 57–78.
Ruggiers, Paul (ed.), *Editing Chaucer: The Great Tradition*, Norman: Pilgrim Books, 1984.
Rüth, Axel, 'Representing wonder in medieval miracle narratives', *Modern Language Notes*, 126 (2011), 89–114.
Sabor, Peter, 'Medieval revival and the gothic', in H. B. Nisbet and Claude Rawson (eds), *The Cambridge History of Literary Criticism: The Eighteenth Century*, vol. 4, Cambridge: Cambridge University Press, 2005, 470–88.
Santini, Monica, *The Impetus of Amateur Scholarship*, Bern: Peter Lang, 2010.
Scala, Elizabeth and Sylvia Federico (eds), *The Post-Historical Middle Ages*, New York: Palgrave, 2009.

Bibliography

Scanlon, Larry, 'Historicism: six theses', *postmedieval FORUM 1: Historicity without Historicism? Responses to Paul Strohm*, October 2011, https://postmedieval-forum.com/forums/forum-i-responses-to-paul-strohm/scanlon/. Accessed 27 May 2013.

Schwyzer, Philip, 'Exhumation and ethnic conflict: from *St Erkenwald* to Spenser in Ireland', *Representations*, 95:1 (2006), 1–26.

Semple, Sarah, *Perceptions of the Prehistoric in Anglo-Saxon England*, Oxford: Oxford University Press, 2013.

Serres, Michel with Bruno Latour, *Conversations on Science, Culture, and Time*, trans. Roxanne Lapidus, Ann Arbor: University of Michigan Press, 1995.

Simpson, James, 'Not just a museum? Not so fast', *Religion and Literature*, 42 (2010), 141–61.

Simpson, James, *Reform and Cultural Revolution: 1350–1547*, The Oxford English Literary History, vol. 2, Oxford: Oxford University Press, 2002.

Smith, D. Vance, 'The application of thought to medieval studies: the twenty-first century', *Exemplaria*, 22 (2010), 85–94.

Smith, D. Vance, *Arts of Possession: The Middle English Household Imaginary*, Minneapolis: University of Minnesota Press, 2003.

Smith, D. Vance, 'Crypt and decryption: Erkenwald terminable and interminable', *New Medieval Literatures*, 5 (2002), 59–85.

Smith, D. Vance, 'The inhumane wonder of the book', *Chaucer Review*, 47:4 (2013), 361–71.

Smithers, Rebecca and Will Woodward, 'Clarke dismisses medieval historians', *Guardian Unlimited* (9 May 2003).

Smuts, Aaron, 'Haunting the house from within: disbelief, mitigation, and spatial experience', in S. J. Schneider and D. Shaw (eds), *Dark Thoughts: Philosophical Reflections on Cinematic Horror*, Lanham: Scarecrow Press, 2003, 158–73.

Soja, Edward, *Postmodern Geographies: The Reassertion of Space in Critical Geography*, New York: Verso, 1989.

Spearing, A. C., 'Interpreting a medieval romance', in Spearing, *Readings of Medieval Poetry*, Cambridge: Cambridge University Press, 1987, 56–84.

Spiegel, Gabrielle, 'Memory and historical time: liturgical time and historical time', *History and Theory*, 41 (2002), 149–62.

Steel, Karl, 'Will wonders never cease: St Erkenwald with claustrophilia', *In the Middle*, 17 November 2009, www.inthemedievalmiddle.com/2009/11/will-wonders-never-cease-st-erkenwald_17.html. Accessed 14 June 2017.

Stevick, Robert D. (ed.), *One Hundred Middle English Lyrics*, Champagne-Urbana: University of Illinois Press, 1994.

Stiegler, Bernard, *Technics and Time: The Fault of Epimetheus*, trans. Richard Beardsworth and George Collins, Stanford: Stanford University Press, 1998.

Strohm, Paul, 'Historicity without historicism?', *postmedieval*, 1 (2010), 380–91.

Strohm, Paul, 'Rememorative reconstruction', *Studies in the Age of Chaucer*, 23 (2001), 3–16.

Strohm, Paul, *Theory and the Premodern Text*, Minnesota: University of Minneapolis Press, 2000.

Summit, Jennifer, *Memory's Library: Medieval Books in Early Modern England*, Chicago: University of Chicago Press, 2008.

Summit, Jennifer, 'Monuments and ruins: Spenser and the problem of the English library', *English Literary History*, 70 (2003), 1–34.

Swales, Peter, 'A fascination with witches: medieval tales of torture altered the course of psychoanalysis', *The Sciences*, 22:8 (1982), 21–5.

Thunø, Erik, *Image and Relic: Mediating the Sacred in Early Medieval Rome*, Rome: L'erma di bretschneider, 2003.

Trigg, Stephanie, *Congenial Souls: Reading Chaucer from Medieval to Postmodern*, Minneapolis: University of Minnesota Press, 2002.

Trigg, Stephanie, 'Introduction: medieval and gothic Australia', in Trigg (ed.), *Medievalism and the Gothic in Australian Culture*, Turnhout: Brepols, 2005, xi–xxiii.

Trigg, Stephanie, 'Medievalism and theories of temporality', in Louise D'Arcens (ed.), *The Cambridge Companion to Medievalism*, Cambridge: Cambridge University Press, 2016, 196–209.

Trigg, Stephanie, 'Once and future medievalism', *antiThesis forum*, 3 (2005), http://pandora.nla.gov.au/pan/66374/20070301–0000/www.english.unimelb.edu.au/antithesis/new2005/forum-3/01-StephanieTrigg.html. Accessed 20 June 2017.

Trigg, Stephanie, 'Walking through cathedrals: medieval tourism and the authenticity of place', *New Medieval Literatures*, 7 (2005), 9–33.

Trilling, Renée R., *The Aesthetics of Nostalgia: Historical Representation in Old English Verse*, Toronto: University of Toronto Press, 2009.

Trilling, Renée R., 'Medievalism and its discontents', *postmedieval*, 2:2 (2011), 216–24.

Tuchman, Barbara, *A Distant Mirror: The Calamitous Fourteenth Century*, New York: Ballantine, 1978.

Turville-Petre, Thorlac, *England the Nation: Language, Literature, and National Identity, 1290–1340*, Oxford: Clarendon Press, 1996.

Twain, Mark, *A Connecticut Yankee in King Arthur's Court*, New York: Carl L. Webster Co., 1889.

Uebel, Michael, 'The pathogenesis of medieval history', *Texas Studies in Language and Literature*, 44 (2002), 47–65.

Utz, Richard, *Chaucer and the Discourse of German Philology: A History of Critical Reception and an Annotated Bibliography of Studies, 1793–1948*, Turnhout: Brepols, 2002.

Utz, Richard, 'The colony writes back: F. N. Robinson's complete works of Geoffrey Chaucer and the *translatio* of Chaucer studies to the United States', *Studies in Medievalism*, 19 (2010), 160–203.

Utz, Richard, 'Coming to terms with medievalism: toward a conceptual history', *European Journal of English Studies*, 15:2 (2011), 101–13.

Bibliography 147

Utz, Richard, *Medievalism: A Manifesto*, Kalamazoo: Arc Humanities Press, 2017.

Valentine, John H. and Kathryn Allen Rabuzzi, 'Holy Anorexia (review)', *Literature and Medicine*, 8 (1989), 167–70.

Vaninskaya, Anna, *William Morris and the Idea of Community: Romance, History and Propaganda, 1880–1914*, Edinburgh: Edinburgh University Press, 2010.

Vaughan, Míceál F., 'The three advents in the Secunda Pastorum', *Speculum*, 55 (1980), 484–505.

Wallace, David (ed.), *The Cambridge History of Medieval English Literature*, Cambridge: Cambridge University Press, 1999.

Wallace, David, *Premodern Places: Calais to Surinam, Chaucer to Aphra Behn*, Oxford: Blackwell, 2004.

Walsham, Alexandra, 'Introduction: relics and remains', in Walsham (ed.), *Relics and Remains*, Past and Present Supplement 5, Oxford: Oxford University Press, 2010, 9–36.

Watson, Nicholas, 'Desire for the past', *Studies in the Age of Chaucer*, 21 (1999), 59–97.

Watson, Nicholas, 'The phantasmal past: time, history, and the recombinative imagination', *Studies in the Age of Chaucer*, 32 (2010), 1–37.

Watson, Steve, 'Touring the medieval: tourism, heritage and medievalism in Northumbria', in Tom Shippey and Martin Arnold (eds), *Appropriating the Middle Ages: Scholarship, Politics, Fraud, Studies in Medievalism*, 9 (2001), 239–62.

Wawn, Andrew (ed.), *Northern Antiquity: The Post-Medieval Reception of Edda and Saga*, Enfield Lock: Hisarlik, 1994.

Weissman, Gary, *Fantasies of Witnessing: Postwar Efforts to Experience the Holocaust*, Itahca: Cornell University Press, 2004.

Wenzel, Siegfried, 'Poets, preachers, and the plight of literary critics', *Speculum*, 60 (1985), 343–63.

Werth, Tiffany J., *The Fabulous Dark Cloister: Romance in England after the Reformation*, Baltimore: Johns Hopkins University Press, 2011.

Wheeler, Bonnie, 'Medieval marketing', *American Book Review*, 31 (2010), 12.

Windeatt, B. A., 'Thomas Tyrwhitt (1730–1786)', in Paul Ruggiers (ed.), *Editing Chaucer: The Great Tradition*, Norman: Pilgrim Books, 1984, 117–43.

Wolfe, Cary, *What is Posthumanism?*, Minneapolis: University of Minnesota Press, 2010.

Woods, William F., *The Medieval Filmscape: Reflections of Fear and Desire in a Cinematic Mirror*, Jefferson: McFarland & Co., 2014.

Žižek, Slavoj, 'Alfred Hitchcock, or, the form and its historical mediation', in Žižek (ed.), *Everything You Wanted to Know about Lacan (But Were Afraid to Ask Hitchcock)*, London and New York: Verso, 1992, 1–12.

Žižek, Slavoj, *The Sublime Object of Ideology*, London and New York: Verso, 1989.

Index

Note: 'n.' after a page reference indicates the number of a note on that page.

abject, the
   in approach to the past 14, 44, 56, 66, 81, 84, 87, 97
   connection to 78–9, 81, 83–6
   medievalism as 8, 13, 16
   viewing the medieval as 10, 14, 16, 22, 52, 55–6, 71, 77–8
academy, the 18, 95, 125–31
   error within 7, 72–4
   within and beyond 14, 23, 70–1, 118–20, 122
   see also humanities; medieval/medievalism
affect
   and medieval objects 2–3, 24, 66, 123–4
   as method 13–17, 61, 76, 97, 105–9, 110–12
   modern-medieval relations and 10, 23, 71, 80, 82, 85, 102–4
   and narratives of the past 24, 37–8, 44
   negative 84, 86–7
   temporalities and 13, 15, 19n.33
amateur medievalism 6–7, 33, 103, 122–3
   in relationship to professional 12, 97–8, 100–1, 104, 108, 113, 125
   see also error; love

amatory 97, 102–3
   neo- 106
   see also love
archive 9, 111, 123–4
   see also memory
Ark of the Covenant 62–5
asynchrony 33–5
   see also Dinshaw, Carolyn; time
Augustine, St 13, 43, 104
authenticity
   desiring 1–2, 59, 73
   questioning 54–7
   representations of 88, 100, 101–2
   see also medieval/medievalism; relics

Bale, John 51
   see also reformers
Baudrillard, Jean 121–2
belief
   as performance 17, 52–4, 57–61, 65–6
   see also objects
Benjamin, Walter 124
Bergman, Ingmar 86–7
Bergson, Henri 12, 20n.53
Bildhauer, Bettina 31, 94n.58, 94n.75
body, the
   abjection and 77, 81–4
   feeling in 61, 110, 111, 113
   as remains 50, 53–4, 56–8

Index

time and 34–5, 39, 49n.73
  see also portal; sleeping; torture
Boccaccio, Giovanni 54
Book of Margery Kempe, The 85, 117n.69
Bynum, Caroline Walker 69n.44, 82, 106, 107, 109

Camille, Michael 124
caritas 104
Catherine of Siena 82–4, 86
Chatterton, Thomas 98–101
Chaucer, Geoffrey
  editing 98–9, 119
  imaginative fiction of 27, 31–2
  Knight's Tale, The 3
  loving 101–5
  Pardoner's Tale, The 54
  reception of 8
  Troilus and Criseyde 31, 45, 105
  voice in works 45, 54
chess 87–8
Christ 64, 84, 90
  coming of 38, 73–4
  on the cross 32, 43
  passion of 111–12, 113
  relics of 50, 69n.51
Christian
  hope 86, 88
  influence 37, 40, 41, 43
  mysticism 110, 112
  pre- 62
  see also Seven Sleepers of Ephesus
Christianity 84
  medieval 76, 86
Civilization and Its Discontents 118
Clarke, Charles 127–8
Cohen, Jeffrey Jerome 13, 32, 68n.38
Commandments 65
community of scholars 128–30
confession 78–80, 87
Connecticut Yankee at King Arthur's Court, A 29
credulity 50, 60, 100

death
  Black 75, 87
  as character 87–8
  dance of 88–9
  fear of 17, 83, 87–90
  space/time and 30, 39, 48n.47, 86
  of the work 45, 91
Decameron 54
Deleuze, Gilles 12, 31
desire
  to get it right 90–1
  to know/inhabit the past 2–5, 9, 15–16, 22, 25–6, 88, 98–102, 106–8, 111, 121–2
  for the object 53, 55, 63, 65–6, 123, 125
  see also Furnivall, F. J.; love; medieval/medievalism; nostalgia; relics; time travel
Dinshaw, Carolyn 109
  amateur vs professional 12, 18n.20, 97, 114n.29
  and emotional connectivity 85, 111
  getting medieval 10–11
  and temporal multiplicity 13, 19n.33, 32–6, 115n.44
  disciplinarity 3, 4, 7, 22–3, 70–5, 95–8, 111, 125–6, 128–30
  post- 14, 120, 126–7, 130–2
discontent
  in accessing the medieval 15–16, 124–5
  disciplinarity and 14, 16, 18, 118, 125, 132
  see also academy, the; Gildas (*De Excidio et Conquestu Britanniae*); *News from Nowhere*
Distant Mirror, A 75–7, 87
Doctor Who 29
Doomsday Book (Willis, Connie) 29
Dream of John Ball, A 16, 26–8, 30
'Dreaming of the Middle Ages' *see* Eco, Umberto

dreams
  abject in 83–4
  Freud's medieval 80–1
  of the medieval 5, 16, 26–9, 30
Dunbar, William 17, 89–90

Eco, Umberto 5–7, 8, 75–6
emotions
  between past and present 23, 36, 71, 81, 89
  disciplinary history of 15, 76
  medieval 83–6, 105–7, 109
  see also affect; feelings; love
error
  character 71–2, 74, 126
  fabulous 50, 52–5
  fear of 17, 70–5, 91, 101, 110, 113
  past cultural 38
  of recognition 77

facsimile 122–5
Faerie Queene 71–2
faery 16, 39–40, 41–2
  see also portal; *Sir Orfeo*; time travel
false
  consciousness 4, 7
  memory 113
  object 50, 52–3, 55–7, 60, 66, 120
  representation 93
  see also authenticity; fantasy; fiction; objects
fantasy
  of Aryan past 6
  disciplinary 74, 95–6, 128
  as limit 80, 82
  lost object 51–2, 65
  portal medievalism 16, 25–7, 31
  recovering the past 4, 7, 14, 62
  see also film; modernity, reconstruction of the medieval; time travel
fear
  and emotional connection to the past 17, 81–3, 121
  see also death: fear of; error: fear of

feelings 15, 131
  abject 16, 82–4
  of discontent 16, 118
  knowing binary 61, 98
  of memory 112–13
  for objects 17, 45
  for the past 13, 38, 76, 85, 101, 107–8, 109
fiction
  medieval imaginative 31–6, 39–44, 53–4
  medievalist writing/films 6–7, 25–6, 28–31, 44, 71, 95, 102
  post-medieval reception/projection 4, 13, 23–4, 26, 51, 61
  /truth 51, 55, 58–9, 80
  see also belief; fantasy; portal: medievalism
film 7, 25, 31, 62, 81, 86–7, 89, 91, 132n.7
Fleming, Juliet 60
Fliess, Wilhelm 78–81
  see also Freud, Sigmund
forgeries 98–101
Foucault, Michel 22, 25
Fradenburg, Aranye 4–5, 49n.76, 51, 65, 106–7, 110, 127, 130
fraud 55, 59, 100
Freud, Sigmund 11, 17, 118
  and the abject 79, 81, 84
  inquisition/psychoanalysis 78–80, 85
Furnivall, F. J. 17, 103–4
  see also love

Game of Thrones 29, 120
Ganim, John 13, 119
Gildas (*De Excidio et Conquestu Britanniae*) 37–9
God
  connection to 109–10
  desire for 88, 107
  love of 85, 115n.33
gothic
  horror 71–2
  medievalism 11, 26, 30, 38, 70, 101

Index

Grail 62, 63
  castle 30
Guantanamo Bay 77–8
  see also torture

Haydock, Nickolas 24, 31, 46n.11, 87, 88, 91
Hirsch, Marianne 112–13
historical studies 1–5, 8, 13, 16, 22–3, 29–30, 44, 52, 54, 61, 63–5, 81, 96, 105, 121
historicism 1–5, 18, 22, 25, 28, 55, 84, 86, 104–5, 119, 121
Hofstader, Richard 129–30
Holsinger, Bruce 8, 9, 18n.19, 119
'How Christ Shall Come' 73–5
humanism/humanists 14, 16, 17, 51–2, 55, 72–3
humanities
  contribution of medievalism to 121
  crisis in 14, 18, 70, 106, 118, 128, 131
  see also academy, the

imaginary
  medieval 24, 29, 45
  medievalist 2, 11, 24, 26, 30, 38, 39, 45, 124
  spatial 24, 106
Indiana Jones 62–3
Ingham, Patricia 4–5, 28, 47n.30
interpretation 17, 70, 72, 104, 113
  anxiety and 70
  no finality in 4
  see also error; forgeries; fraud

Johnson, Samuel 99–100
Julian of Norwich 109, 111–12, 113
  see also love

Kempe, Margery 17, 32, 36, 85–6, 110, 115n.44
knights see Connecticut Yankee at King Arthur's Court, A; Faerie Queene; film; Seventh Seal, The; tourism: dark
Knight's Tale, A 9
know/ing 59, 89, 103, 126
  desire to 25, 88
  feeling and 61, 98
  unknowing/unknowable 16, 17, 40, 60, 107
  ways of 126, 130
  see also belief; feelings; wonder
Kristeva, Julia 81, 83

Latour, Bruno 12, 32
Leland, John 51, 109
Lerer, Seth 45, 71–3
Levine, Joseph 55
Lion, the Witch and the Wardrobe, The 16, 29, 47n.28
Lord of the Rings, The 29
loss/finding 51, 62–5, 91, 121
love
  of God 85, 110, 115n.33
  medievalist 101–4, 122–3, 132
  for the past 4, 14–15, 97–8
  in rhetoric of affect 104–9
  see also desire; Walpole, Horace

magic
  of objects 16–17, 24, 47n.29, 66
  storytelling/communication as 16, 106–7, 109–10
  see also wonder
Malo, Robyn 54
Mann, Jill 105
manuscript
  connection to 102–3
  context 74
  fictional medieval 30, 58, 99–100
  as trace of the past 9, 13, 24, 96, 98
  see also fascimile
Massey, Doreen 35
Matthews, David 7, 18n.19, 45, 46n.4, 114n.9, 132n.2
Medieval Academy of America 6

medieval/medievalism 3, 5–8, 10–11, 13, 35–6, 80, 109, 111
  disciplinary boundaries 71, 75, 95–6, 120–1
  and discontent 14, 16, 118, 125, 132
  fixity vs interpretative 22–4
  mutually constitutive/continuous 23, 42, 44–5, 86, 119–20, 124–5
  as simulacrum 121–2
  through true/false relics 50, 55–6, 100–1
  see also amateur medievalism; community of scholars; facsimile; modernity (relationship to the medieval)
medieval studies
  and affect 15–16, 61, 76, 97, 106
  anxiety in 70–1, 75, 95
  future of 4, 17, 118, 127, 130–2
  and medievalism 3, 6–8, 13–14, 23, 26, 95–6, 111, 119–21, 125
  professionalisation of 97–8, 104
  see also medieval/medievalism
medievalist
  affect/emotions 45, 87, 102–3, 106, 109
  cinema 7, 25, 31, 62, 71, 81, 86–7, 89, 91, 119
  imaginary 2, 11, 24, 26, 30, 38–9, 45, 124
  nineteenth century 26–7, 31, 103
  professionals 71–2, 74, 100–1, 104, 122, 124
  temporality narratives 23–4, 26, 29–31, 36
  thinking/practice 3–8, 11–18, 22–3, 85, 91n.1, 95–6, 111, 118–22, 131
  within the academy 127–8, 130
  within the medieval 38–45
  see also fiction; neomedievalism; relics; white supremacy
melancholia 51, 53, 109, 116n.48, 128

memory
  affective history and 49n.73, 111–13
  destroying 51–2
  repressed/recovered 79–80
Middle Ages, the
  abject 11, 16, 52, 77, 81–2, 86
  affective approach to 2–3, 15, 17, 97, 102, 106, 108, 113
  Freud and 78–81
  inventing/reinventing 3–8, 13, 22–3, 30, 75–7, 87, 96, 109
  as self-reflective 32, 36–9
  space of 10–11, 14–15, 22–6, 29, 32, 36, 64, 74–5, 105, 128
  see also Distant Mirror, A; fantasy; modernity (relationship to the medieval); Seventh Seal, The
miracle(s)
  narratives 68n.37
  relics and 53
  temporal 35, 50
  see also wonder
modernity (relationship to the medieval) 87, 96, 118, 128
  and abjection 14, 17, 44, 52, 77–8, 81–3, 85
  affect and 101–5, 107–8
  belief in temporal/spatial difference 11–12, 15, 23–5, 29–31, 44, 50, 70, 97
  and desire 3, 23–4, 26, 131
  making the Middle Ages 7, 32, 40, 43
  and memory 112–13
  post 8–9, 18, 121–2
  reconstruction of medieval 3, 8, 16, 22, 45, 98–100, 123–4
  similarity with medieval 9, 11, 76–8, 82–3, 85
  verifying of truth 55, 61
  see also neomedievalism; portal; time; time travel
monasteries 53, 57
  dissolution of 51–2
  see also reformers

Index

Monty Python and the Holy Grail 77, 82
mood
　collective 61, 66, 118
　histories attentive to 17
　in poetry 105
Morris, William
　domestic medievalism 2, 27
　dream of the medieval 26, 28–9, 30
　neo-medievalism 26, 41
mystery plays 32
　see also Christianity

neomedievalism 8–9, 15, 122, 131
News From Nowhere 26, 28, 30
Northern Homily, The 33
nostalgia 6, 9, 14, 37, 44, 72, 80, 101, 121–2, 128, 130

objects
　belief in 17, 66
　of desire 4–5, 63, 122
　loss/finding 51–3, 62, 65
　love/desire for 15, 103, 121
　power of 2, 17, 24, 30, 36, 50, 53–4, 56, 59–60, 62–4, 124
　subject and 8, 66, 82, 97, 101, 103, 107
　see also relics; sacred
oldness 1–3, 10, 24, 50, 102
　see also facsimile; relics

Parker, Matthew, Archbishop of Canterbury 51, 52
Patrimonio 123–4
Patterson, Lee 70–1, 104–5
Pearsall, Derek 1–3, 40
Piers Plowman 31
pleasure
　in the abject 81, 85
　of discovery 4, 23
　through the object 65
　see also desire; love
portal
　medieval 39–42

medievalism 16, 29–31, 36, 47n.28
post-medieval, the 55, 119, 131
　affect 17, 66
　and the medieval 24, 37, 38, 51
　recreation/invention 2, 3, 17, 22, 45
Protestantism 51–2, 56, 72
　see also reformers
Pulp Fiction 10

Readings, Bill 128, 130
Reformation 51, 55–6
　post- 61
reformers 50–2, 53, 55–6, 58
relics 17, 24, 50–60, 62–6, 99, 126
　see also authenticity; objects; reformers
remains 39, 53, 55–6, 65, 96
Renaissance
　antiquarian approach 26, 68n.33, 71–2
　and dark Middle Ages 36, 52
　humanism 14, 16
representation
　accurate 52, 59, 88, 96
　complicating 60, 62, 64, 121
　of medieval past 1, 5, 9, 26
Rising (1381) 1, 27
romance
　genre 30, 51, 53, 62–3
　see also Sir Orfeo
Rowley, Thomas 98–100

sacred
　space/object 31, 54–7, 63, 66, 69n.51, 84
St Erkenwald 43, 57
science
　historiographical 55
　and time travel 25, 29
scientia 60, 104
Semple, Sarah 38–9
Serres, Michael 20n.50, 32, 49n.65
Seven Sleepers of Ephesus 33–6
Seventh Seal, The 82, 86–9, 90, 94n.75

shame 84–5
Simpson, James 51–2, 107–8, 111, 119
Sir Gawain and the Green Knight 41, 44, 53
Sir Orfeo 16, 39–42, 43
sleeping 26–8, 33–6, 39
  see also time
Smith, D. Vance 9, 11, 91, 107–8, 111, 119, 133n.19
space
  disciplinary 95, 130
  interior 61, 106
  medieval 24–6, 29–30
  medieval notions of 31, 34–5, 37, 39–42, 45
  and time 15, 22, 26–8, 58
Spenser, Edmund 8, 71–2, 126
Spiegel, Gabrielle 112
Strohm, Paul 2, 4–5, 32, 60, 69n.60, 112

temporal pleating 10, 32, 41–2, 89
temporal switching 31, 36, 42–3
temporality/ies
  affective 15, 19n.33
  amateur 114n.29, 125
  medieval 16, 29, 31–45
  medieval as prior 15, 22, 124
  multiple/layered 2, 10, 12–13, 97, 108
  and recuperation 8, 24, 59
  and space 26–8, 30
  see also portal; time travel
terror
  of death 89
  about error 71
  self-loathing and 87
time 8, 11–13, 97, 107, 112
  emotion and 16, 85, 103, 124
  futurity and 84, 86–8, 90–1
  medieval 29, 31–45
  objects and 2, 63
  and space 10, 15, 22, 58

  see also time travel
Time Machine, The 25
time travel 13, 23–31, 36, 44, 113, 124
  medieval 31, 33–6
  see also portal
torture 10–11, 77–81, 84, 85
touch/ing
  affect and 17, 24
  of God 65
  manuscript facsimile 123–4
  the medieval 2–3, 8, 13, 16
tourism
  cultural/heritage 24–5
  dark 44, 85, 92n.29
Très Riches Heures of the Duc de Berry 123–5
Trilling, Renée 19n.33, 37, 48n.54
Trotula, The 34
Troy 31, 43–4
truth
  discernment of 1, 66, 77–81
  and error 52–3, 55, 71–2, 74, 113
  and fiction 4, 7, 50–1, 57–9, 60–1
  search for 121, 128, 130
  see also abject, the; memory
Tuchman, Barbara 75–7, 87
Twain, Mark 26, 29, 30
Tyrwhitt, Thomas 98–101

uncanny, the 11–12, 33, 49n.76, 77

Wallace, David 13, 106–7, 109, 110
Walpole, Horace 17, 100–3
Walsham, Alexandra 53, 65
Warton, Thomas 99–100, 106
Watson, Nicholas 106–8, 109–11
Wells, H. G. 25–6
Wenzel, Siegfried 74
white supremacy 5–6
witches 75, 79–80, 85
wonder 59–61, 66
  see also objects

EU authorised representative for GPSR:
Easy Access System Europe, Mustamäe tee 50,
10621 Tallinn, Estonia
gpsr.requests@easproject.com

www.ingramcontent.com/pod-product-compliance
Lightning Source LLC
Chambersburg PA
CBHW070239240426
43673CB00044B/1852